THE BRIDGESTONE

100 BEST
PLACES TO STAY
IN IRELAND 2001

JOHN McKENNA - SALLY McKENNA

ESTRAGON PRESS

FIRST PUBLISHED IN 2001

BY ESTRAGON PRESS

DURRUS

COUNTY CORK

© ESTRAGON PRESS

TEXT © JOHN & SALLY McKENNA

THE MORAL RIGHT OF THE AUTHORS HAS

BEEN ASSERTED

ISBN 1 874076 37 5

PRINTED IN IRELAND

BY COLOUR BOOKS LTD

THE BRIDGESTONE
100 BEST PLACES TO STAY IN IRELAND 2001

WRITTEN BY JOHN McKENNA

CONTRIBUTING EDITORS:

ORLA BRODERICK

ELIZABETH FIELD

PUBLISHING EDITOR: SALLY McKENNA

EDITOR: JUDITH CASEY

ART DIRECTION BY NICK CANN

COVER PHOTOS BY MIKE O'TOOLE

WEB: FLUIDEDGE.IE

FOR DERMOT O'BRIEN

WITH THANKS TO...

Colm Conyngham, Des Collins, Brian Condon

Frieda Forde, Sile Ginnane, Conor Cahill

Paul Willoughby, Ian Vickery

Bernadette O'Shea, James O'Shea, Paula Buckley

Kevin and Benedict Connolly

Margie Deverell, Lelia McKenna

Judith Casey, Maureen Daly, Colette Tobin

Nick Cann, Pat Young, Maurice Earls

Mark and Millie Deverell

Mike O'Toole, Ann Marie Tobin

BRIDGESTONE

...is the world's largest tyre and rubber manufacturer.

◼ Founded in Japan in 1931, it currently employs over 95,000 people in Europe, Asia and America and its products are sold in more than 150 countries. Its European plants are situated in France, Spain and Italy.

◼ Bridgestone manufacture tyres for a wide variety of vehicles from passenger cars and motorcycles, trucks and buses to giant earthmovers and aircraft.

◼ Many Japanese and European cars sold in Ireland have been fitted with Bridgestone tyres during manufacture and a host of exotic sports cars including Ferrari, Lamborghini, Porsche and Jaguar are fitted with Bridgestone performance tyres as original equipment.

◼ Bridgestone commercial vehicle tyres enjoy a worldwide reputation for superior cost per kilometre performance and its aircraft tyres are used by more than 100 airlines.

◼ In 1988 Bridgestone acquired the Firestone Tyre and Rubber Company combining the resources of both companies under one umbrella. This, coupled with an intensive research and development programme, has enabled Bridgestone to remain the world's most technologically advanced tyre company with testing centres in Japan, USA, Mexico and Italy.

■ Bridgestone tyres are distributed in Ireland by Bridgestone/Firestone Ireland Limited, a subsidiary of the multinational Bridgestone Corporation. A wide range of tyres are stocked in its central warehouse and staff provide sales, technical and delivery services all over Ireland.

■ Bridgestone tyres are available from tyre dealers throughout Ireland.

FOR FURTHER INFORMATION:

BRIDGESTONE/FIRESTONE IRELAND LTD
Unit 4
Leopardstown Office Park
Dublin 18
Tel: (01) 295 2844
Fax: (01) 295 2858

34 Hillsborough Road
Lisburn
BT28 1AQ
Tel: 028 926 78331

website: www.bridgestone-eu.com

THE 10th ANNIVERSARY ISSUES

Two hugely important changes have taken place during the ten years that we have written the annual Bridgestone 100 Best Guides, both of them changes for the better.

Firstly, the standards evident amongst the best places to eat and stay have risen steadily and inexorably.

Secondly, the whole concept of discussing food and drink and places to stay, the whole idea that this is a topic worthy of discussion and argument, the belief that it forms a major part of our cultural life and is worthy of serious analysis and intellectual enquiry every bit as much as our political culture or our artistic culture, is now firmly rooted in the national psyche.

The rise in standards has been gratifying, indeed thrilling, and has been the main reason why Ireland's food culture is now discussed in terms which compare it to the most exciting food cultures in the world.

The sheer passion which the best Irish cooks now articulate for their work is intoxicating, and they have been fortunate to have seen that passion matched by an appreciative audience who value and respect their work. No good customers, no good cooks, it is as axiomatic as that.

And this relationship between cook and customer has resulted in this vital dialogue that leads to a true depth of cultural value in the business of cooking and offering hospitality. Ireland has changed from a country which excused its shortcomings by virtue of its insularity, and been transformed into a place where international influences are hungrily seized upon in order to be learnt from and assimilated.

And the dialogue has extended further, then, to embrace the media and to address the question of what is truly important in a food culture, what is truly of value. Of course, we still have throwbacks who believe that you discuss a restaurant by telling people what you ate and whether you liked it or not, and who report on food matters from the comfort of a hotel suite with a gin 'n' tonic in one hand and a press release in the other.

This brain-dead nonsense will always endure, sadly, but its impact is truly marginal today, for the smart consumer who spends their money wisely and who thinks with concern about the issues of food and food production and food quality doesn't listen to this arrogant megalomania. Instead, they demand that you explain and inform them to the best of your ability, and that modest aim has been the intention of the Bridgestone 100 Best Guides during the past decade.

At times the books have provoked controversy, and whilst this has on occasion been unpleasantly vituperative, we have welcomed it as a chance to bring the vital issues of food and quality into the mainstream of debate, and to put forward our own methods of deciding what is truly of value.

It is perhaps worth reflecting on how those methods have been refined over ten years of writing. We first discovered the food culture which has since dominated our lives back in the late 1980's. What we valued about it was its concentration on the art and craft of food and hospitality. It wasn't obsessed with success in a material sense, but rather with doing the job as well as it could be done.

All the trappings with which other people surrounded the business of food and hospitality was largely irrelevant to these people: for them it was a personal journey. They had to do their best – no matter how simple the situation, or how unlikely it was – and in doing their best we found that they produced the best food, and created the best environment in which we could enjoy ourselves and appreciate their work. We looked for the meaning, the philosophy, which underpinned what they did, and we found it in abundance.

This approach is commonplace today, but for many years it proved iconoclastic, and we were regarded as some sort of foodie cranks, weirdos who hammered on and on about organic foods, and artisan skills, and the craft of cooking which could make it a great art. We found the people we respected in the most unlikely places, but again for some folk this merely proved that we didn't understand that what happens in the metropolis must always be more important than what is going on out in the sticks.

But what we have seen during the last decade has convinced us that great food and great hospitality always comes from the heart, and that you cannot fix a label or a location on anyone or any place and decide that this makes it more or less important. Grandness does not mean goodness. Simplicity does not imply second place. Ireland's food and hospitality culture is a culture of individuals and individualism, people who work to their own métier. As they have grown in confidence over the last ten years, they have actually become emboldened, and have dared to make their work simpler, truer, and more personal. Our books salute their efforts, because we respect them and the journey they have made, the journey that they have taken us upon. They have made Ireland's culinary culture and its culture of hospitality one of the most interesting, most quixotic and most fascinating of any in the world.

JOHN & SALLY McKENNA
DURRUS, CO CORK

- **The Bridgestone Icons** are those hosts and places that offer the most outstanding hospitality and the most stylish houses.

- **The Bridgestone Classics** are those hosts and places that have contributed significantly to Ireland's culture of hospitality.

- **The Bridgestone New Wave** are those hosts and places to stay with the greatest potential to contribute to Ireland's culture of hospitality.

THE ICONS

COUNTY CORK
Assolas House, Kanturk
Fortview House, Goleen
Longueville House, Mallow

COUNTY GALWAY
Norman Villa, Galway
Quay House, Clifden

COUNTY KERRY
Shelburne Lodge, Kenmare

COUNTY LIMERICK
The Mustard Seed at Echo Lodge, Ballingarry

COUNTY WATERFORD
Buggy's Glencairn Inn, Glencairn

COUNTY WEXFORD
Kelly's Resort Hotel, Rosslare
Salville House, Enniscorthy

THE CLASSICS

COUNTY CARLOW
Kilgraney Country House, Bagenalstown

COUNTY CORK
Ballymaloe House, Shanagarry
Ballyvolane House, Co Cork
Seven North Mall, Cork

COUNTY DONEGAL
Ardnamona, Lough Eske

COUNTY DUBLIN
The Clarence, Dublin
The Morgan, Dublin

COUNTY KERRY
Allo's Townhouse, Listowel
The Park Hotel, Kenmare
The Sheen Falls, Kenmare

COUNTY MAYO
Newport House, Newport

COUNTY MONAGHAN
Hilton Park, Clones

COUNTY SLIGO
Temple House, Ballymote

COUNTY WATERFORD
Hanora's Cottage, Clonmel
Richmond House, Cappoquin

COUNTY WESTMEATH
Temple Country House, Horseleap

THE NEW WAVE

COUNTY CORK
Glenally House, Youghal
Grove House, Schull

COUNTY DONEGAL
The Mill Restaurant & Accommodation, Dunfanaghy

COUNTY GALWAY
Dolphin Beach, Clifden

NORTHERN IRELAND
The Moat Inn, Templepatrick

HOW TO USE THIS BOOK

■ The Bridgestone 100 Best Places to Stay in Ireland is arranged **ALPHABETICALLY, BY COUNTY** so it begins with County Carlow, which is followed by County Clare, and so on.

■ Within the counties, the entries are once again listed alphabetically, so Aherne's, in Youghal, East Cork, is followed by Assolas House, in Kanturk, North Cork.

■ Entries in Northern Ireland are itemised alphabetically, at the end of the book. All NI prices quoted in sterling.

■ The contents of the Bridgestone 100 Best Guides are exclusively the result of the authors' deliberations. All meals and accommodation were paid for and any offers of discounts or gifts were refused.

■ Many of the places featured in this book are only open during the summer season, which means that they can be closed for any given length of time between October and March. Many others change their opening times during the winter.

■ **PRICES:** Average prices are calculated on the basis of one night's stay for bed and breakfast. Look out for special offers for weekends, several days' stay, or off season.

■ **CREDIT CARDS:** Most houses take major credit cards, particularly the Visa, Access/Master group. Check if you intend to use American Express or Diners Card. If a house does not accept credit cards, this is indicated in the notes section of their entry.

■ Finally, we greatly appreciate receiving reports, suggestions and criticisms from readers, and would like to thank those who have written in the past, whose opinions are of enormous assistance to us when considering which 100 places to stay finally make it into this book.

CONTENTS

BARROWVILLE TOWNHOUSE
Randall & Marie Dempsey
Kilkenny Road, Carlow, Co Carlow
Tel: (0503) 43324 Fax: 41953
www.barrowvillehouse.com

Barrowville is a handsome Victorian house, white painted and set behind a tall wall at the roadside just as the main Carlow road leaves the town and begins to head south to Kilkenny. Randall and Marie Dempsey both have backgrounds in the hotel business, which bestows them with a calm confidence, but nothing is taken for granted in their work, and their efficiency and consideration are considerable. They are true professionals – confident and capable, sure of how to achieve what they want to achieve. The public rooms are grand, and successfully achieve that aura of welcome and comfort which encourages you to sit down with some tea and a brain candy magazine and let the cares of the world wash over you. And those who dislike the suburban style which is so dominant in Ireland will appreciate the restraint used in the downstairs rooms: they are classic.

The bedrooms, on two floors, are of various sizes, with those at the top of the house smaller and more compact than the spacious rooms on the first floor. The decoration here is rather busy, but successful within its own ambitions, and it creates a comfortable house which has an intimacy in spite of its size.

Breakfast is taken in the conservatory at the side of the house, and along with a fine selection of cereals, fruits, cooked meats and cheese from a buffet, the traditional breakfasts are excellent – properly cooked with good ingredients. Barrowville strikes an interesting note between the formality of a country house hotel and the personality of a B&B, and does it rather well, which means it is a place with its own character.

- **OPEN:** All year
- **ROOMS:** Eight rooms, all en suite
- **AVERAGE PRICE:** B&B £25-£27.50 per person sharing, £30-£35 single room rate

- **NOTES:**
No dinner. No Wheelchair Access. Enclosed car parking
Children – over 12 years welcome
- On right after the traffic lights heading south out of Carlow.

KILGRANEY COUNTRY HOUSE ©
Bryan Leech & Martin Marley
Bagenalstown, Co Carlow
Tel: (0503) 75283 Fax: 75595 kilgrany@indigo.ie
www.kilgraneyhouse.com

Kilgraney is one of the great houses, and here is why. 'You'll be happy to learn that there are not too many changes from last year', says Bryan. 'Well, we have a new dining room which we'll open at the start of the season. And we have re-worked, re-decorated and re-styled our breakfast room, and we're really happy with the way the room has turned out. Oh, and we hope to launch our self-catering apartments later in the year, so restorations to barns, stables and tack rooms are on-going. And in July and August we will be opening for dinner for non-residents on Thursday, Friday and Saturday nights.'

So, there you go. For a dynamic duo like Bryan and Martin, that torrent of work, that avalanche of achievement, amounts to 'not too many changes'. Blimey! That's why Kilgraney is so good, so admired, so respected, dammit, so well loved. The style of Kilgraney is sublime – the house has been a regular in several style magazines over the past years – and the hospitality is true, and the people you meet here always seem especially interesting, especially fascinating. And Bryan Leech is a fine cook, with a culinary style as distinctive as his design sense: medallions of pork with a dried cherry and balsamic sauce; hot prawn and salmon mousseline with a lemon and caper sauce; dark chocolate pudding with an orange and cardamom sorbet. It breaks your heart to leave, so it does. But you will be back, have no fear. Everyone comes back, but everyone.

● **OPEN:** Mar-Nov, weekends, mid-Jun-Aug weekly
● **ROOMS:** Six double rooms, en suite
● **AVERAGE PRICE:** £35-£55 per person sharing, £15 single supplement

● **NOTES:**
Dinner 8pm, £28, communal table, book by noon
Vegetarian and special diets catered for with notice
No Wheelchair Access. Enclosed car parking
Children – under 12 by arrangement only
● Just off the R705, 3.5 miles from Bagenalstown (Muine Bheag) on the road heading towards Borris.

LORD BAGENAL INN
James & Mary Kehoe
Leighlinbridge, Co Carlow
Tel: (0503) 21668 Fax: 22629
info@lordbagenal.com www.lordbagenal.com

It is one of life's delights, being a customer in The Lord Bagenal.

Even if you only drop in for a pint of beer in the bar, you feel welcome, comfortable, cared-for. The staff are a delight: unclichéd, generous with their chat and their time, concerned that you should get the very best out of the Lord Bagenal, whether your visit is for dinner and a few days r'n'r, or if you have just pulled off the road to grab a bite of lunch.

There are 12 rooms and they are comfortable, thoughtful and well-composed spaces, just the sort of place to hide away to on Friday evening after a stressful week in Dublin. In the future, as the marina on the river is further developed and mooring for more boats is created, this will become a refuge for sailors and what could be nicer than to drift down to Bagenalstown, moor the boat, then have dinner and overnight here? Ah, the sweet life.

James Kehoe is a complex man, but a clue to what drives him might be glimpsed by taking a close look at the terrific art collection he has amassed quietly and patiently, and also at the very carefully collected and annotated wine list. Both are distinctive and thought-provoking, and indeed in all aspects of his work Mr Kehoe is looking to create something singular and special. He succeeds, thanks to excellent staff who are with him every inch of the way, producing delicious and enjoyable cooking for dinner and breakfast, and thanks especially to his ability to be a true inn keeper: courteous, genuine, hospitable.

- ● **OPEN:** All year, except Christmas
- ● **ROOMS:** Twelve rooms, incl. family rooms, & suite
- ● **AVERAGE PRICE:** B&B from £35 per person sharing, £10 single supplement

- ● **NOTES:**
Restaurant open 8am-midnight
Vegetarian options always available
Wheelchair Access
Children – welcome (family rooms, playground)
- ● Seven miles from Carlow, off the N9.

CLIFDEN HOUSE
Jim & Bernadette Robson
Corofin, Co Clare
Tel: (065) 6837692 Fax: 6837692

They are good craic, the Robsons, and they are humorous people, too, in a sardonic, unclichéd way, with an appreciation of the absurdity of things which makes the lovely Clifden House all the more vital and vivid.

'We offer a particularly individual welcome and are not associated with any register or guide,' they write, and those are just the sort of qualities that make them a perfect subject for an idiosyncratic guide like the Bridgestone, and makes their house the perfect destination for an independent minded person just like yourself. There is an original independence of mind about Jim and Bernadette Robson, and their fine, romantic house in this lovely, rolling part of County Clare.

Their bohemianism is best expressed by an approach to design and to furnishing that is truly refreshing – the style of Clifden is unlike anywhere else, and the fact that the restoration continues apace, bit by bit, is actually a thrill – you feel as they work on the house that you yourself all the better appreciate Clifden. Jim and Bernadette have been bringing Clifden back from the brink of ruin for years now, succeeding in taking the house, built around 1750, some way into the modern age. Its location, with Lough Inchiquin hard by, and the River Fergus flowing through the grounds, is magical, creating a sense of being in the very heart, the very soul, of the country.

Tellingly, they write that 'Clifden House is an echo from another time – a time when life was larger, when hospitality was king and his subjects were more important than his possessions.'

- **OPEN:** Mar-mid Dec
- **ROOMS:** Four rooms, all en suite
- **AVERAGE PRICE:** B&B £35-£38 per person

- **NOTES:**
Dinner 8pm, £25, communal table
Enclosed car parking
No Wheelchair Access
Children – welcome, cot, high chair
- Left of the grotto in the village, second right, then first right into the drive.

FERGUS VIEW
Mary Kelleher
Kilnaboy, Corofin, Co Clare
Tel: (065) 683 7606 Fax: 683 7192 deckell@indigo.ie

'The warmest of welcomes. Lots of advice given, but in a tactful and unobtrusive way', wrote some travellers after they had navigated their way all around the country with a Bridgestone guide, with a stay in County Clare just south of the Burren at Mary Kelleher's splendid B&B, Fergus View, a mile or so outside the village of Corofin.

What else was there to praise? The evening meal, which brought forth an exclamated 'Excellent!' What about breakfast then? Same again: 'Excellent!'

That's how everyone responds to Mrs Kelleher's helpful hospitality. The warmth of the welcome and the succulent and satisfying cooking more than compensate for the fact that the rooms in Fergus View are relatively small by modern standards. But this is an old house, so don't expect the acreage which you will find in purpose-built guesthouses which are littered around the county.

No, what you will find, and what matters in Fergus View is the solicitous care and the instinctive generosity of Mrs Kelleher. She is a good cook because she loves to cook, and she gets a real kick out of bringing a wonderful dinner together: perfect curried parsnip soup; rich mushroom and tarragon crepe; toothsome chicken with a mushroom and white wine sauce which restores the soul; great Burren lamb with rosemary and garlic in the classic style, and then smashing puddings: lovely lemon geranium leaves with rich lemon cheesecake; smashing pear and frangipane tart; to-die-for pavlova. A bottle of wine, a comfortable bed upstairs, bliss! Reach for those exclamation marks yourself! Breakfast is just as good as dinner.

- **OPEN:** 1 Apr-30 Sept
- **ROOMS:** Six rooms, five en suite
- **AVERAGE PRICE:** £24 per person sharing
£10-£12 single supplement

- **NOTES:**
No credit cards. Dinner 6.30pm, book by noon, Mon-Thur, £17. Advance notice appreciated for vegetarian, special diets. Enclosed car parking. No Wheelchair Access. Children – high chairs, cot, babysitting. No smoking.
- The house is 2 miles north of Corofin, on the left hand side, 100m from Kilnaboy Medieval church.

ADELE'S

Adele Connor
Adele's Bakery, Schull, Co Cork
Tel: (028) 28459 Fax: 28865
adele@adelesrestaurant.com
www.adelesrestaurant.com

Adele's little tea rooms and restaurant with rooms, in the glamorous, clamorous little village of Schull, is one of those happy places which resists change.

This is not because change frightens Ms Connor. Far from it. Like so many Cork folk, Adele Connor is a restless soul, always looking to improve things slowly, steadily.

No, they don't change things – the simple style of the public rooms for eating on the first two floors, the simple style of the four bedrooms for staying in on the third floor at the top of the house – because the way they are works perfectly, and the way they are has a modest aesthetic which is charming.

These are not grand rooms – the four of them share a landing at the top of the house (which was a bank, once upon a time) and they share a single bathroom with a shower. But if you are youthful in spirit, these rooms will be evocative and perfectly suitable. They may bring you right back to your salad days, backpacking and winging it by the seat of your pants as you travelled the globe, full of energy and inquiry, staying in pensiones here and there. Whatever age you are, you will love the smell of baking and the aroma of coffee rising from the bakery in the early morning, and you will love the thought that after a day spent exploring the peninsula, you can return to Adele's to enjoy some highly individualistic cooking in the restaurant, and you will love also the simple correctness, the politesse, with which Adele and her staff do things. They do them right and, because of that, they don't need to change.

● **OPEN:** Easter-Halloween, Christmas & New Year
● **ROOMS:** Four rooms, sharing one shower-room
● **AVERAGE PRICE:** B&B £20 per person

● **NOTES:**
Bakery, Café open all day, Dinner Easter & high summer 7pm-10.30pm, £20. Vegetarians & vegans welcome
No Wheelchair Access. Children – welcome
● On the main street in Schull, at the top of the hill.

10 GREAT BREAKFASTS

①
ANGLESEA TOWNHOUSE
CO DUBLIN

②
THE CLARENCE HOTEL
CO DUBLIN

③
FERGUS VIEW
CO CLARE

④
FORTVIEW HOUSE
CO CORK

⑤
HANORA'S COTTAGE
CO WATERFORD

⑥
HILTON PARK
CO MONAGHAN

⑦
MADDYBENNY FARMHOUSE
NORTHERN IRELAND

⑧
McMENAMIN'S TOWNHOUSE
CO WEXFORD

⑨
THE OLD WORKHOUSE
CO MEATH

⑩
SHELBURNE LODGE
CO KERRY

AHERNE'S

The Fitzgibbon family
163 North Main Street, Youghal, Co Cork
Tel: (024) 92424 Fax: 93633
ahernes@eircom.net   www.ahernes.com

They never stop, the Aherne family. Like the other great Cork families who work in the hospitality business, they are driven by a relentless need to develop and improve. And so, virtually every year since they first opened their rooms to guests, as a complement to their famous restaurant and pub, there has been a new project, a new diversification, all the better to improve the splendid food and hospitality environment which they have created in Youghal for three generations now.

It may seem hard to believe, but it's not so long ago now, that Aherne's was a fairly straightforward bar and restaurant. Today, there are no fewer than a dozen rooms, all beautifully and luxuriously and distinctively furnished, and a new small conference/private dining room is another smart and welcome development.

The Aherne's rooms are special because in addition to being superlatively comfy and stylish, they are very large – five of them are in effect mini-suites – whilst the others are also built on a much-larger-than-normal scale.

But the Aherne family's implicit understanding of just what the traveller needs means that the rooms are blissfully cosy and exceptionally thoughtful. Wisely, given that the house has no views other than from the rooms at the front onto the narrow main street, the rooms are little empires unto themselves, the swaddle you up in their grand comfort.

And staying here means you get to enjoy David Fitzgibbon's splendid fish cookery in the restaurant, not to mention the excellent and original bar food served in the bars.

● **OPEN:** All year
● **ROOMS:** Twelve rooms, all en suite
● **AVERAGE PRICE:** B&B £55-£85 per person sharing, £80-£85 single

● **NOTES:**
Dinner Mon, Sun 6.30pm-9.30pm Mon-Sun, £33
Bar food served all day, Sun Lunch
Private car parking. Full Wheelchair Access
Children – welcome, high chair, cot, babysitting
● Well signposted as you approach Youghal.

ASSOLAS COUNTRY HOUSE

Joe & Hazel Bourke
Kanturk, Co Cork
Tel: (029) 50015 Fax: 50795
assolas@eircom.net www.assolas.com

Hazel Bourke's cooking in Assolas House defines what country cooking means, and demonstrates precisely what it can achieve, in the modern age.

Here is a cook whose work is without artifice, whose sole culinary strategy is to unveil and express the inherent, intrinsic flavours of food. If that sounds like an obvious thing to say, then remember that today, for many chefs, cooking has become the practice of pure artifice; working with indifferent ingredients, they seek to use any means to give them flavour.

Hazel Bourke doesn't do that. Instead, her quest for culinary purity presents the diner with food of almost naked simplicity: a St Tola goat's cheese custard with a roasted tomato sauce sees her at work with one of the great Irish farmhouse cheeses, whilst one of her other favourite cheeses, Bill Hogan's superlative extra-hard Gabriel cheese, forms the dressing for a salad of garden greens.

Like other smart, young, modern cooks, Mrs Bourke keeps her menus short and her choice of ingredients pitched to perfection. Glistening white hake is baked with aged balsamic vinegar and olive oil and garden herbs. Kenmare mussels are served with catriona potatoes from the garden. Kanturk sirloin of beef is roasted, and served with garden vegetables.

If this food is peerless, then the subtle and beautiful aesthetic of Assolas House itself is the perfect place in which to enjoy it. This is a disarmingly special house. Joe Bourke's hospitality is as charming as his wife's cooking is convincing, and together they make Assolas a little jewel.

● **OPEN:** Mid Mar-Nov
● **ROOMS:** Nine rooms, all en suite
● **AVERAGE PRICE:** B&B £60-£85 per person sharing

● **NOTES:**
Dinner 7pm-8pm, £30
Vegetarian and special diets welcome, with notice
No Wheelchair Access. Enclosed Car Parking
Children – welcome, high chair, cot, high tea
● Take the N72 Mallow/Killarney Road, and 10km west of Mallow you will see the first signpost.

BALLYMAKEIGH HOUSE
Margaret Browne
Killeagh, Co Cork
Tel: (024) 95184 Fax: 95370
ballymakeigh@eircom.net
http://homepage.eircom.net/~ballymakeighhouse

Margaret Browne has become a restaurateur, as well as a celebrated B&B keeper, with the opening of her restaurant, Browne's, just a couple of miles east of her long-established farmhouse B&B, Ballymakeigh House, and close to the N25.

It's an idea which she had been planning for many years now, and no one should have doubted that this relentless woman would not have realised her ambition.

Browne's is a handsome, purpose-built restaurant with two main rooms, both spacious and comfortable, and the cooking is well realised and pleasing. It is a valuable addition to the area, though it does make one ask just how one woman can manage to run two establishments. But, if any woman can, Mrs Browne can.

Ballymakeigh continues as before, thanks to the fact that Mrs Browne has assembled an excellent team in the house. It is a comfortable place, part of a working dairy farm, and offers lots of things for the sporty-minded to do, as well as a good space to simply do little or nothing. The only difference in the working arrangements is that guests can – and usually do – choose to eat at Browne's at dinner time, and transport can be arranged for those who don't wish to drive.

But Ballymakeigh remains Margaret Browne's great achievement, a welcoming, comfortable house, with fine cooking at breakfast, and it is a perfect place from which to explore the beauties of East Cork and the region.

● **OPEN:** Mar-Nov
● **ROOMS:** Six rooms, all en suite
● **AVERAGE PRICE:** B&B £35 per person sharing, £45 per person single

● **NOTES:**
Dinner available in Browne's Restaurant (transport arranged, if required). No Wheelchair Access
Enclosed Car Parking
Children – welcome, high chair, cot, babysitting
● Signposted on the N25, 6 miles west of Youghal.

BALLYMALOE HOUSE ©
The Allen family
Shanagarry, Midleton, Co Cork
Tel: (021) 465 2531 Fax: 465 2021
res@ballymaloe.ie   www.ballymaloe.ie

There is no other theatre quite like it. The drawing room at Ballymaloe, before dinner, makes for fascinating viewing. There is the judge with his rather embarrassing wife. There are the well-heeled European travellers, in internationally branded clothing and accessories. There are the cultured Americans, admiring the art and speaking softly. And there, speaking louder than anyone else, is a group of young Irish people. They are well dressed, but their clothing suggests people who work. Their clothes are straightforward and functional, rather than the glitzy this-takes-money look of the Europeans. They are laughing, discriminatingly ordering the right apéritifs. Their huge confidence is striking. They are articulate, intelligent, comfortably moneyed, keyed in to the language of food, socially at ease. This is Ireland's dot.com generation, and they've chosen Ballymaloe to spend their largesse.
So why do they come to Ballymaloe?
The answer is because Ballymaloe represents something more than just a weekend break, a destination with nice food in the beautiful countryside of East Cork. Myrtle and Ivan Allen have created an icon address that stands for something more. It stands for what Mrs Allen calls the 'civilised achievement' that is appreciating good food and wine, good art and beautiful countryside, the rich culture which these things together can bring to us. Other places are grander, plusher, but Ballymaloe is a modern classic because its attractions are timeless. Old money or new money find it irresistible, for the simple reason that it civilises us all.

- **OPEN:** All year except 24-26 Dec
- **ROOMS:** Thirty three rooms, all en suite
- **AVERAGE PRICE:** B&B £67.50-£85 per person sharing, £15 single supplement

- **NOTES:**
Dinner 7pm-9.30pm, £37.50
Wheelchair Access. Enclosed Car Parking
Children – welcome, high chair, cot, babysitting
- Well signposted from Midleton.

BALLYVOLANE HOUSE ©

Merrie & Jeremy Green
Castlelyons, Fermoy, Co Cork
Tel: (025) 36349 Fax: 36781
info@ballyvolanehouse.ie
www.ballyvolanehouse.ie

You could apply all sorts of nicey-nicey terms to Ballyvolane, but such nicey-nicey talk would risk overlooking the steely professionalism which Merrie and Jeremy Green bring to their métier and to this grand house. These are meticulous, hard-working folk, whose attention to detail is genuinely inspiring.

If you can, for example, get into the dining room ahead of everyone else at breakfast time or dinnertime, and just look at the faultless arrangement of the big dining room table, the militaristic precision with which cutlery and crockery and decorations have been placed. It is always beautifully executed and it makes the heart sing to see such care and such importance placed on a vital detail which all too many people overlook these days.

If the heart sings with the detail, the tummy positively sings with the food. Working with her main chef, Maeve, Merrie Green produces expressive and delicious cooking: strongly flavoured consomme; fine fillet of salmon with prawns and gorgeous garden fresh vegetables; superb raspberry meringue cake. It is just the right food: comforting yet exactingly executed, the sort of cooking that animates the conversation around the big table.

The Greens finish the magic of Ballyvolane by being superlatively helpful and hospitable, and their work makes this one of the most enjoyable of the grand country houses. For fishing, for walking, for chilling out away from the stresses of the capital, Ballyvolane is hard to beat.

● **OPEN:** All year, except Christmas
● **ROOMS:** Six rooms, five en suite
● **AVERAGE PRICE:** B&B £40-£50 per person sharing, £15 single supplement

● **NOTES:**
Dinner 8pm, £26, communal table
Wheelchair Access. Enclosed Car Parking
Children – welcome, high chair, cot
● From the N8, south just after Rathcormac, take the turn to Midleton and look for the sign for the house.

BANTRY HOUSE

Brigitta & Egerton Shellswell-White
Bantry, Co Cork
Tel: (027) 50047 Fax: 50795
bantry@hidden-ireland.com

'A great experience, which cannot really be compared to anywhere else,' wrote a traveller after a couple of nights' stay in Bantry House.

And yes, it truly is an imposing place, a memorable place, high on the hill overlooking Bantry Bay. It's unforgettable to stay here for a couple of days, even given the fact that one actually stays in a wing of the house, and not in the main body of the house itself.

This section of the house is largely devoted not merely to an exhibition space for the furniture and art works of this magnificent mansion, but it also hosts concerts and a week-long chamber music festival each June, which is regarded by critics as the finest music festival in Ireland. As a location for listening to chamber music, the library is simply sublime.

The house has been owned by the White family since 1739, and has been open to the public for more than 50 years. In recent times, Egerton and Brigitta Shellswell-White have concentrated considerable energies on the gardens, and one must-do thing when you stay here is to clamber up the 'stairway to the sky' at the rere of the house: the views from the top of this massive climb of steps is extraordinary.

The six rooms and one suite are all very lushly appointed, and what we love is the feeling the house bestows of being completely immersed and abandoned in such restrained luxury. Even though the house hosts thousands of visitors each year, you are unaware of them when you stay here. Bantry really can't be compared to anywhere else.

● **OPEN:** 1 Mar-Oct 31
● **ROOMS:** Six rooms, one suite, all en suite
● **AVERAGE PRICE:** B&B £75-£85, per person sharing £10 single supplement

● **NOTES:**
Dinner for groups, please enquire when booking.
No Wheelchair Access. Enclosed Car Parking
Children – welcome, high chair, cot, babysitting
● East side of Bantry town, at the harbour.

BARNABROW COUNTRY HOUSE

Geraldine O'Brien
Cloyne, Midleton, Co Cork
Tel: (021) 4652534/4652776 Fax: 4652534
barnabrow@eircom.net
www.barnabrowhouse.com

One wonders where on earth Geraldine O'Brien gets the energy to accomplish all that she does at Barnabrow. Ever since the O'Briens took over this fine house, dating from the early seventeenth century, a whirlwind of activity has been taking place.

The house itself has been beautifully converted for guests, with subtle and romantic rooms that are a style lover's delight: these really are very tactile hideaways and the colours and furnishings are beautifully imagined and realised with powerful individuality.

But there is also an organic garden, a wildlife sanctuary, a posse of pets and animals including a pair of donkeys, and The Ironwoods shop which sells African furniture which is recycled from teak railway sleepers – the same furniture which is so forcefully and effectively used in the house itself.

In addition to the Trinity Rooms restaurant, where local man Eamon Harty is chef, there are a pair of small conference rooms, a number of excellent guest rooms at the rere of the main house, and Geraldine's latest plan is a language and culture school.

Others would baulk at such a torrent of work, but Mrs O'Brien simply gets on with it and achieves whatever she puts her mind to. Her great achievement, above all, has been to make Barnabrow such a special place, such a distinctively stylish address, such a fine place to stay.

● **OPEN:** All year, except Christmas
● **ROOMS:** Twenty one rooms, all en suite
● **AVERAGE PRICE:** B&B Main House £47.50 per person sharing, Courtyard £33 per person sharing, single supplement £10

● **NOTES:**
Mor Chluana Restaurant serves dinner.
Wheelchair Access. Enclosed Car Parking
Children – playground, donkeys, ducks, hens & geese
● From N25, turn right at Midleton roundabout, follow signs for Cloyne. 1.5miles from Cloyne, Ballycotton Road.

BLAIR'S COVE HOUSE
Philippe & Sabine De Mey
Durrus, Bantry, Co Cork
Tel: (027) 61041 Fax: 61487
blairscove@eircom.net

'I think the rooms at Blair's Cove are immensely stylish,' wrote a friend who spent a couple of summertime days staying in the house.

Indeed they are. In their intelligent use of design and the good fortune that is their outstanding location, the accommodation here reveals both the beauty of the detail, and the utter gorgeousness of the grander canvas. The grand canvas, then, is the house's incredible location on a promontory jutting out into the lovely Dunmanus Bay. The vistas across the Sheep's Head peninsula and the Beara peninsula are awesome, the quietude of the bay itself and its wonderfully unspoilt aspect a balm for the soul. Mark Rothko might have painted its great bands of colour: shining blues, fern-red hills, goat's hair skies, and he might almost have been able to capture their mesmeric beauty.

Inside the houses and apartments – which are arranged around and about the restaurant, and which can be rented for self-catering or taken for shorter periods when you can avail of bed and breakfast – Philippe and Sabine De Mey show the beauty of the detail.

They have an expert idea for colour and contrast and comfort, so whilst the different spaces vary wildly, they are united by an expert appreciation of how to make a space welcoming. Do note that there is also a lovely stone cottage, a few miles down the road at Goleen pier, which can also be rented, and its location is every bit as spectacular as the main house.

● **OPEN:** All year
● **ROOMS:** Available for both B&B and self catering.
● **AVERAGE PRICE:** £45-£75 per person sharing, £15 single supplement

● **NOTES:**
Restaurant open Tue-Sat (Mon also during Jul & Aug), Dinner £31. Restaurant closes end Oct-mid Mar
Children – high chair, cot
● 1.5 km outside the village of Durrus on the Barleycove/Mizen Head road. Look for the blue gates.

BOW HALL
Dick & Barbara Vickery
Castletownshend, Co Cork
Tel: (028) 36114

You meet Barbara Vickery and you think to yourself: this woman has just walked out of a kiddies' storybook.

There she is, bow-tie bright, with those kind, giggly-granny eyes, a little bundle of thoughtfulness and concern. For more than twenty years she has been running this lovely house, and yet she dances about the place like a child, not like someone who has already celebrated fifty happy years of marriage.

There are only three bedrooms in this fabulous house, and of course they all have names: the Apricot Room, the Toffee Room and the Oak Apple Room.

The style mixes Shaker with a nod to the Arts & Crafts school, and it is an intensely family home: lots of wedding portraits and family snaps lining the walls, some nifty Oscar Peterson buzzing away in the background, a sitting room and library which looks like it has just walked out of a Frank Capra movie. Super cosy.

It is just the right house to be in when staying in this most delightful of villages. Made famous by the writers Somerville and Ross, who lived here, Castletownshend is not only picture book perfect, it has one of the steepest streets in the country, and the street has a tree in the middle of it.

Mrs Vickery's breakfast muffins, quickly concocted at breakfast-time, are already quietly famous in Ireland, and one soft sweet mouthful will explain just why. She also makes a dynamite homemade sausage, and light pancakes drizzled with maple syrup, and she even cuddles your kid whilst you eat and chat and have a wonderful time.

- **OPEN:** All year, except Christmas
- **ROOMS:** Three rooms, all with private baths
- **AVERAGE PRICE:** B&B £35 per person sharing, £5 single supplement

- **NOTES:**
No Smoking House. No Credit Cards accepted
Dinner 8pm, £24, communal table
No Wheelchair Access. Enclosed Car Parking
Children – welcome, high chair, cot
- Right hand side of the village heading down the hill.

BUTLERSTOWN HOUSE

Elisabeth Jones & Roger Owen
Butlerstown, Bandon, Co Cork
Tel: (023) 40137 (business/fax) Tel: 40524 (guest phone, pay phone), www.butlerstownhouse.com mail@butlerstownhouse.com

Butlerstown is gorgeous. The house was built by Jonas Travers around 1805, designed by an architect by the name of Hutchinson, and together Travers and Hutchinson concocted a tone poem of Georgian architecture, a work of art in stone, plaster and wood.

The proportions of the house are magical, not least the bifurcated staircase which would repay hours of study alone. Hutchinson and Travers knew a thing or two about light, so the tall windows, and the huge window framing the stairs, flood the house with light. The day rooms, with their grand fireplaces, are elegant, and Lis Jones and Roger Owen show their discrimination with the sparseness of their furnishings: no clutter here, instead a leanness which is almost minimalistic and which showcases and frames every detail of the house to perfection.

And the details could be pored over for hours: the plasterwork with its starfish and scallops and rope motifs; the false window on the exterior; the clever use of furniture which shows Roger Owen's craft as a furniture restorer. The Georgians, with their eye for balance and effect, were minimalists centuries before Bauhaus, and Butlerstown is one of the most decisive essays in the art of simplicity and good judgement which you will find.

If the house creates a marvellous feeling of well-being thanks to its aesthetic, and the enviable location of the house ties up the pleasure points to perfection, the hospitality of Jones and Owen completes the picture. They are ebullient and fun and they enjoy their work, and you will most certainly enjoy their stunning house.

● **OPEN:** Mar 15-Oct 31
● **ROOMS:** Four rooms, all with private bathroom
● **AVERAGE PRICE:** £45-£55 per person, £10 single supplement

● **NOTES:**
Dinner for house parties, if taking whole house, one week's notice. No Wheelchair Access. Enclosed Car Parking. Children – over 12 welcome. No smoking
● Signposted clearly from Butlerstown.

FORTVIEW HOUSE

Violet Connell
Gurtyowen, Toormore,
Goleen, West Cork
Tel: (028) 35324 Fax: 35324

If we had a fiver for every time we have been told that Fortview House is 'the finest B&B I have ever stayed at', we could retire tomorrow and live on truffles and ortolans and start collecting Jack Yeats paintings.

Well, we don't have that fiver, of course, but what we have heard over the years has been simply the most amazing torrent of praise for the hospitality and housekeeping of Mrs Connell.

Everyone loves everything about this house, set hard by the road from Durrus to Goleen, a few miles north of the latter village, a perfect base for exploring the Schull, Sheep's Head and Beara peninsulas of West Cork. The breakfasts are amongst the finest in the country – hot potato cakes with crème fraîche and smoked salmon; poached, scrambled and fried eggs 'laid by our happy lazy hens'; fresh juices and cereals, pancakes and scones and kippers and black and white pudding: the entire kaleidoscope of breakfast possibilities is offered here.

If breakfast is great, dinner is even better, offering 'a starter; a home-made soup of the evening; a main course of what is available fresh on the day, from our farm and our garden and my local producers'. Some local farmhouse cheeses will follow, then dessert, then some tea or coffee to conclude. And then a blissful night in the comfort of these stylish rooms in this stylish house. You wake up in the morning and feel that you are in the B&B made in heaven. You are.

- **OPEN:** 1 Mar-1 Nov
- **ROOMS:** Five rooms, all en suite
- **AVERAGE PRICE:** B&B £25-£30 per person sharing £10 single supplement

- **NOTES:**
Dinner, £20 (book by noon)
Self catering house available, sleeps six
No Wheelchair Access. Enclosed Car Parking
Children – over 6 years welcome
- Signposted 2km from Toormore on the main Durrus road (R591). 12km from Durrus, 9km from Goleen.

10 HOUSES NEAR THE MAJOR ROADS, FERRIES & AIRPORTS

①

BALLYTEIGUE HOUSE
CO LIMERICK (SHANNON AIRPORT)

②

ECHO LODGE
CO LIMERICK (SHANNON AIRPORT)

③

GARNISH HOUSE
CO CORK (CORK AIRPORT & FERRIES)

④

IVYLEIGH HOUSE
CO LAOIS (N7)

⑤

LEGENDS GUESTHOUSE
CO TIPPERARY (N8)

⑥

McMENAMIN'S TOWNHOUSE
CO WEXFORD (ROSSLARE FERRY)

⑦

THE MOAT INN
NORTHERN IRELAND (INTERNATIONAL AIRPORT)

⑧

PRESTON HOUSE
CO LAOIS (N8)

⑨

SEVEN NORTH MALL
CO CORK (CORK AIRPORT & FERRIES)

⑩

SIMMONSTOWN
CO DUBLIN (DUBLIN FERRIES & AIRPORT)

GARNISH HOUSE

Con & Hansi Lucey
Western Road, Cork City, Co Cork
Tel: (021) 427 5111 Fax: 427 3872
garnish@iol.ie   www.garnish.ie

There have been acres of newsprint and hours of broadcasting time devoted in recent years to discussing the negative effects of The Celtic Tiger, as Ireland's economic boom has been tagged. It seems, according to some Dublin-based commentators, that we have stopped being a nation of folk with all the time in the world to talk and have a pint with strangers and visitors, and have instead become rude and uncaring. A little bit of cash, it seems, has transformed us all into people who behave with the brusqueness of Parisians.

Anyone who knows that this is not true, and who wants proof positive that it is not true, should just book into Garnish House for a night. And there, in the person of Hansi Lucey, you will find the embodiment of everything that is true, real, genuine, inimitable, caring, solicitous, painstaking, natural, unaffected, generous and spirited about Irish hospitality. Mrs Lucey is the veritable business, the real article, the full shilling, of what hospitality in Ireland is all about. She and her staff don't just look after you in Garnish – they effectively take you under their wing, take you into their care. Garnish is a big Victorian house on the Western Road heading out of Cork city, and it looks pretty much like all the other big Victorian houses along here which have been converted into B&B's.

But, thanks to Hansi, it isn't like the others. Nothing is too much trouble for this lady and her staff, no request too arcane or awkward. They live and breathe the most special hospitality in the world, and no Celtic Tiger, howsoever powerful, could change them a jot.

● **OPEN:** All year
● **ROOMS:** Fourteen rooms, all en suite
● **AVERAGE PRICE:** B&B £35-£45 per person sharing £35-£55 single

● **NOTES:**
No Dinner (many local restaurants). 30 choices for breakfast! Wheelchair Access. Enclosed Car Parking
Children – welcome, high chair, cot, babysitting
● Five minutes' walk from city centre, just opposite UCC.

GLENALLY HOUSE ❷

Fred & Herta Rigney
Copperally, Youghal, Co Cork
Tel: (024) 91623
enquiries@glenally.com www.glenally.com

The only problem with Fred and Herta Rigney's gorgeous Glenally House, a mile or so out of Youghal, is as follows. If you stay in the lilac room, then you get to enjoy the superb design and style features of the room which this couple have eclectically and energetically collected from all over the world. Smart and sassy lighting. Great use of colour. A feeling of pure, individual, aesthetic.

But then you don't get to enjoy the superb design and style features of the green room, with its smart little shower room and glass brick wall. And, of course, you won't have had a chance to try the exotic, 19th century Spanish metal bed in the room at the front of the house, not to mention the fabulous quilt which adorns it, and the glamorous curtains – look at the width of those stripes! – which the Rigneys have made for the room. But then, if you do get to slumber there, you miss out on the ingenious style of the blue room which adjoins it.

And that's the problem, in a nutshell.

Of course there will be time to enjoy the breakfast room and the sitting room and the dining room, but given that each room in this lovely house has its own unique design, then the only way to win out in the design stakes is to stay for four nights and book a different room each night. Like the best houses, Glenally has been gifted with a style which complements and animates this early 19th-century merchant house. The Rigneys use a confrontational aesthetic, mixing old and new pieces with an acuity of eye which is superb. This house is an aesthete's dream, and happily the hospitality matches the owner's passion for design.

● **OPEN:** All year. Reservations only Nov-Feb.
● **ROOMS:** Five rooms, all en suite
● **AVERAGE PRICE:** B&B £25-£40 per person sharing, £10 single supplement

● **NOTES:**
Dinner, £24, Light meals available. No smoking
No Wheelchair Access. Enclosed Car Parking
Children – no facilities for very young children
● Five minutes' walk – and signposted – from town centre.

GROVE HOUSE ◊
Billy & Mary O'Shea
Colla Road, Schull, Co Cork
Tel: (028) 28067 Fax: 28069
billyoshea@yahoo.com
www.cork-guide.ie/schull/grove/welcome.html

By choosing to stay in Grove House you will join a list that, in the past, has included George Bernard Shaw, Jack B. Yeats and Edith Summerville. This building has had and seen many lives, and today it's in the welcoming hands of Mary and Billy O'Shea, who have seized the opportunity to restore it and once again offer hospitality.

Grove House sits up proudly on Schull's poshest boulevard (and believe us, Schull is posh), the much sought-after Colla Road, where the many new and restored buildings all overlook the harbour, and yet feel a part of this buzzy little town.

Billy and Mary are meticulous characters who have carefully and suitably decorated this house in a wash of glorious colours. Downstairs one room is lined with panels from an old bank, the fireplace even has a letterbox for you to post your lodgements, and a bar has been fashioned from two corner pieces of the sturdy woodwork. The bank panelling shows up again upstairs, this time used as a bedhead, with the final two remaining panels cleverly made up as doors for two bedside tables. Each bedroom is different, with a careful selection of artworks that have obviously been collected over time.

It's a relaxing place. People choose to sit long over breakfast which Mary makes to order using the great West Cork foods, Gubbeen bacon, and Sally Barnes' smoked fish. How many, we wonder, speculate on the conversation that could have taken place in this very room amongst Shaw, Yeats, and Summerville.

● **OPEN:** All year. Reservations only Nov-Feb.
● **ROOMS:** Five rooms, all en suite
● **AVERAGE PRICE:** B&B £35-£40 per person sharing, £10 single supplement

● **NOTES:**
No Dinner. No smoking
No Wheelchair Access. Enclosed Car Parking
Children – not suitable for very young children
● Five minutes' walk – and signposted – from town centre.

LARCHWOOD HOUSE
Sheila & Aidan Vaughan
Pearson's Bridge, nr Ballylickey, Co Cork
Tel: (027) 66181

Larchwood House has the reputation of offering the best cooking in the area, thanks to Sheila Vaughan's ambitious and ultra-professional skills.

Mrs Vaughan has an impressive culinary CV and dinner in Larchwood leaves one in no doubt whatsoever about her abilities.

A roast duck salad with salad leaves and ginger shows the sort of globalisations she enjoys and with which she is thoroughly comfortable and well in control, though for the most part the cooking is solidly classical. She makes a superb chicken and chive soup, or perhaps a carrot and coriander soup; she makes the very most of a gratin of cod topped with breadcrumbs; whilst loin and fillet of lamb is both hugely ambitious and is perfectly cooked and presented. Her shellfish cookery is assured – scallops with tomato and basil hits the spot, and even a rarity such as woodcock, cooked during its very short season, is done magnificently. Portions are enormously generous, and service is amiable and relaxed, though some object that the style of the room is very domestic.

The rooms are comfortable, all en suite and offering very good value for money, and Larchwood is an excellent base for touring the West Cork peninsulas, especially with the promise of a good dinner at the end of a day's touring, and the fact that one only needs to pop upstairs means that extra bottle of wine has your name on it.

Keen gardeners should note that if Mrs Vaughan is mistress of the kitchen, Mr Vaughan is master of the garden, and this fine garden is actually part of the West Cork Garden Trail.

● **OPEN:** All year
● **ROOMS:** Four rooms, all en suite
● **AVERAGE PRICE:** B&B £28 per person

● **NOTES:**
Dinner 7pm-10pm, £26
No Wheelchair Access. Enclosed Car Parking
Children – over 6 years welcome
● Turn off the N71 at Ballylickey and take the Kealkil Road for approximately 2 miles.

LONGUEVILLE HOUSE

The O'Callaghan family
Mallow, Co Cork
Tel: (022) 47156 Fax: 47459
info@longuevillehouse.ie longuevillehouse.ie

Hospitality is instinctive for the O'Callaghan family. What they have, they share. Their lovely old house. Their generous natures. Their exquisite food. As the following story demonstrates.

One day we accompanied William O'Callaghan on a visit to some of his local suppliers. After the exotic mushroom growers, we visited a fruit farm, where the owner also presented us with a couple of combs of honey. Back in Longueville, William told his mother, Jane, that he had been given a gift of the honey. 'Wonderful!', she said. 'We'll put it out in the morning for the guests' breakfast, that's the best honey you can get!' Typical.

Allied to this generosity is a degree of self-sufficiency in Longueville which is daunting. It is their own lamb which turns up on the plate, and most of the vegetables you will enjoy have come from no further than their own gardens. Salmon will have been hoisted from the Blackwater river. A small collation of wine is made every year. This is an important factor, for William O'Callaghan is one of the greatest cooks in the country.

The house is pink and handsome, the public rooms are grand and noble, the dining room bedecked with portraits of the presidents of Ireland, and the bedrooms are sumptuous without being in the slightest bit overblown. With the intuitive, gracious hospitality of the family, their generosity with time and care, it makes for one of the greatest Irish houses, a place where everything is done in the style of the O'Callaghans, and is thereby done with truly great style, and generosity.

- **OPEN:** Early Feb-17 Dec
- **ROOMS:** Twenty rooms, all en suite
- **AVERAGE PRICE:** B&B £63-£125 per person sharing, £40 single supplement

- **NOTES:**
Dinner, 6.30pm-9pm, £36-£48. House parties off season No Wheelchair Access. Enclosed/Locked Car Parking Children – welcome. Winter breaks. Conference Centre
- 4 miles west of Mallow on the N72 to Killarney.

THE OLD BANK HOUSE
Marie & Michael Reise
11 Pearse Street, Kinsale, Co Cork
Tel: (021) 774075 Fax: 774296
oldbank@indigo.ie   http://indigo.ie/~oldbank

In the world of hospitality, one is usually fearful when you hear that someone running a successful business has decided to 'expand'.

More often than not, such an act is a prelude to declining standards and service, as a shortage of staff (an endemic problem in Ireland which seems to be getting ever worse) and the ever greater demands of more work means that things begin to go wrong.

Well, one might dread to hear it, but for smart people like Michael and Marie Reise, who have been involved in the restaurant and hospitality business in Kinsale for many years now, the extension last year of their handsome townhouse up to a complement of 17 rooms, was handled painlessly, and served only to modernise, up-grade and improve this vital address in the busy resort town of Kinsale.

The Reises use a muted palette of colours throughout the house, soft greys, greens and yellows, a delicate touch which adds to the luxurious feel of the Bank House. Overall, though it seems curious to say it, one is most impressed here by the understatement, the confident feeling that comfort will speak for itself and that nothing needs to shout for attention.

The public rooms are for relaxing and, at breakfast time, they are cosy. All told, The Old Bank House is a model of professionalism, a vital asset in a town which is frequently far too frothy for its own good. Kinsale, by the way, is best seen at respectively the beginning and the end of the season, when it is not too hectic with visitors.

- ● **OPEN:** All year, except Christmas
- ● **ROOMS:** Seventeen rooms, all en suite,
- ● **AVERAGE PRICE:** from £120 per room

● **NOTES:**
No Dinner (many restaurants locally)
Wheelchair Access – three steps to door, but elevators inside. No private parking
Children – welcome, but house not suitable for toddlers
● Beside the Post Office in the centre of Kinsale.

SEA COURT
David Elder
Butlerstown, Bandon, Co Cork
Tel: (023) 40151

David Elder describes his work on the beautiful Sea Court house as involving 'time and love', and as anyone who has ever set out to restore a Georgian mansion will know, you need both of those qualities, in massive and plentiful abundance, along with a heap of money.

Mr Elder's restoration is as painstaking as his hospitality. Most recently he has repainted the ballroom of the house in a vibrant blue, in order to make it more vividly colourful.

Indeed, the colours used in Sea Court are of major importance – all the bedrooms are named after the colours they are painted – as they capture not merely the period nature of the house, but also succeed in being a vital component of the fascinating and arresting light which is such a feature of this area of west Cork. If you ever felt like you wanted to take a painting holiday, this would be one of the places where the light would fascinate any painterly eye: pack up that easel!

Mind you, it can be difficult to drag yourself out of doors, for Sea Court is such a beautiful, such a grand, old house that it's tempting to linger here all the day long. A good lazy breakfast seems merely to set you up for a snooze, but do go and have a stroll around the newly cleared two-acre orchard near the house. You can amble around and nibble fruit from the trees and, perhaps, immerse yourself in biblical thoughts. Like the fact that you must, you just must, be in some sort of garden of Eden, here in Sea Court, walking in the sunshine and thinking already about dinner in this genial house.

● **OPEN:** 8 Jun-20 Aug
● **ROOMS:** Six rooms, all en suite, or with private bath
● **AVERAGE PRICE:** B&B £25-£30 per person

● **NOTES:**
No Credit Cards accepted
Dinner if pre-booked. Self catering Sept-May
No Wheelchair Access. Enclosed Car Parking
Children – welcome, high chair, cot, babysitting
● From Timoleague, cross the bridge, then turn left in front of the Abbey. Travel just over 2 miles.

SEA VIEW HOUSE HOTEL
Kathleen O'Sullivan
Ballylickey, Co Cork
Tel: (027) 50073 Fax: 51555

'I think Sea View is the best hotel I have ever stayed in anywhere.'

A good friend of ours, who stayed in Kathleen O'Sullivan's lovely hotel during the week of the West Cork Chamber Music Festival, said this to us, spontaneously, without a jot of exaggeration.

What makes it the best? Simple, really. They care for you, they look after you. 'I asked for an ironing board, and it wound up that they did my ironing!,' said our friend.

And that's the kind of thing they do: if they can do anything for you, then they will do it. Fixing a sandwich. Food for the kids. Doing the ironing. Cooking something to your liking for dinner. It doesn't matter what. Ms O'Sullivan and her team are dedicated to the noble calling of hospitality, which means this ageless hotel sails on serenely, unaffected by fashions, demonstrating the trueness and timelessness of real hospitality.

Just as typically, whilst Ms O'Sullivan could rest on her many laurels, she refuses to do so. A building project during the winter has added a new wing to the hotel, containing a pair of suites and five new rooms, and the dining room has also been extended. The hotel is bigger, but it remains as intimate as ever.

The hot tip in the dining room is to choose their classic steak garni for dinner. It's the sort of timeless dish which they do to perfection: a melting sirloin that invigorates like nothing else, and which always makes those who did not order it say, 'Oh, I wish I had ordered that', and which makes you say, 'You know, I think this is the best...'

● **OPEN:** Mid Mar-mid Nov
● **ROOMS:** 25 rooms, all en suite, 1 wheelchair access
● **AVERAGE PRICE:** B&B £50-£60 per person sharing £15 single supplement; special rates by request

● **NOTES:**
Dinner 7pm-9pm, £25-£27.50, Sun Lunch £14 +10%sc
Full Wheelchair Access. Car Parking
Children – welcome, high chair, cot, babysitting by arrangement
● 3 miles west of Bantry on the N71 Glengariff road.

SEVEN NORTH MALL ©
Angela Hegarty
7 North Mall, Cork
Tel: (021) 439 7191 Fax: 430 0811
sevennorthmall@eircom.net

It's such a civilised place, Seven North Mall.

For us, you see this vital quality at its best at breakfast time. Here is a meal which Angela Hegarty and her team elevate to the status of simple greatness, by virtue of the precision of each detail. Juices and fruits and cereals are fresh and appetising. The eggs are so fresh and golden, so expertly scrambled. The bacon is sweet and salty. The bread and toast are both superb, the coffee a rich, good brew.

The cutlery and crockery are gleaming and tactile, well chosen to add greater pleasure to the meal.

There are the broadsheet newspapers to peruse, and a calm atmosphere in the breakfast room, with deft, gentle service. It sets you up for the day like no other breakfast, simply because it gives you a little bit of calm before you face the day.

And that is what Seven North Mall is all about, and why it has such a cult reputation. It's an oasis of calm. It may be very close to the centre of Cork city, but being on the North side of the quays means the stretch of the waterway is peaceful. The rooms are understated and very comfortable, but they have all you need. Staying here means you need only to stroll in to some of the best restaurants in the city – Café Paradiso: Jacob's on the Mall; 5 Fenn's Quay are some that are a few minutes' walk away. And there is even a microbrew pub just a few doors down the quay, with excellent beers made on the premises. There is no more perfect base, and no more civilised place.

- **OPEN:** All year, except Christmas
- **ROOMS:** Seven rooms, all en suite
- **AVERAGE PRICE:** B&B £35-£40 per person sharing. £10 single supplement

- **NOTES:**
No Dinner (numerous local restaurants)
Wheelchair Access. Locked Car Parking
Children – over 12 years welcome
- City centre, north bank of north channel of River Lee

THE WEST CORK HOTEL
John Murphy
Ilen Street, Skibbereen, Co Cork
Tel: (028) 21277 Fax: 22333
westcorkhotel.com info@westcorkhotel.com

Virtually every Cork address featured in this book has carried out significant improvements, changes, developments and what-have-you over the last couple of years, and John Murphy of The West Cork Hotel is no exception. Restless people, unstoppable people, folk who blaze a trail for everyone else, and who explain why Cork stays ahead of the rest.

Having upgraded many of the bedrooms in recent years, major design changes have recently been visited with great success on the dining room and the function room on the ground floor. Louis Calleja did the design work, and it's pure classic. The transformation of the dining room, in particular, seems somehow to have retained the charm of the old room whilst being able to make it more plush and better lit, more contemporary yet completely timeless. It's a great piece of work.

And the other great work in the West Cork is the service by a great team of people working with Mr Murphy. These people look after you so well, even if you are doing no more than grabbing a bite to eat in the bar at lunchtime, and their welcome is so hospitable it puts you at your ease instantly.

People love The West Cork Hotel in the same way that you love a treasured object which is significant and meaningful to you, and you alone. It's like a favourite teddy, or a favourite painting, even a favourite poem. Every time you return to it, you find new depths, new pleasures.

● **OPEN:** All year, except Christmas
● **ROOMS:** Thirty rooms, all en suite
● **AVERAGE PRICE:** B&B £40 per person sharing, £10 single supplement

● **NOTES:**
Dinner 6pm-9.30pm Mon-Sun, from £16.50
No Wheelchair Access. Enclosed Car Parking
Children – welcome, high chair, cot
● Follow the N71 in the one way system out of Skibbereen, heading towards the West and the hotel is just before the Kennedy bridge as you leave town.

ARDNAMONA HOUSE ©
Amabel & Kieran Clarke
Lough Eske, Donegal, Co Donegal
Tel: (073) 22650 Fax: 22819
ardnamona.com info@ardnamona.com

They probably invented the term 'idiosyncratic' in order to describe Ardnamona and Kieran and Amabel Clarke, who own this gorgeous house. They are witty, wilful, and as unclichéd as people can be, and as such they breed the spirit that animates this splendiferous house, they positively orchestrate it with their hospitality. Sometimes it can seem that you cannot find a better match, in terms of owners and house. They belong here.

Ardnamona, though only a few miles west of Donegal town, feels splendidly out of time. And so, with their slightly other-worldly air, do its owners, their understated manner and manners, their utter lack of commercialism a breath of fresh air in our relentless modern world. The Clarkes create a true sense of escape, and as you edge along Lough Eske and then turn down the hill into the long drive through the grounds of the house – celebrated for its extraordinary collection of tree rhododendrons – you seem to simply leave the world behind.

The house, which now enjoys a small musical theatre where concerts are held, and where you will find a marvellous old Steinway once played by Paderewski, is decorated with restraint and a wise appreciation of colour and suitability. Ardnamona is ever-so-slightly grand, and yet somehow it is also intimate, it is welcoming. There is nothing discordant in this house, and the welcome, the style, the setting, the cooking – Mrs Clarke cooks very well indeed – all create the perfect atmosphere.

● **OPEN:** All year, except Christmas
● **ROOMS:** Six rooms, all with private bathrooms
● **AVERAGE PRICE:** B&B £40-£47 per person sharing, £10 single supplement

● **NOTES:**
Dinner Mon-Sat 8.30pm, £20, communal table. Booking essential. Enclosed car parking. No Wheelchair Access Reservations essential
Children – welcome, high chair, cot, babysitting
● Leave Donegal on N15. After 5kms take small turning on left marked Harvey's Point.

CROAGHROSS

John & Kay Deane
Portsalon, Letterkenny, Co Donegal
Tel: (074) 59548 Fax: 59548
jkdeane@croaghross.com www.croaghross.com

Have you ever had a problem with PWT?
Don't take offence if that seems like an inordinately private and eerily probing question. PWT can strike anyone: male; female; young; old. It's a difficult condition, but more common than folk care to admit. Of course, a lot of people simply brush it off, and say it's got nothing to do with them, thanks all the same. They are deluding themselves. PW. is Post-Wedding Trauma. We have all been there.

And what on earth has that got to do with Croaghross. Simple. Folk suffering from PWT (exhausted mothers, impoverished fathers, guests with 3-day hangovers) have begun to find that a spell in John and Kay Deane's superb Croaghross Cottage is the perfect cure for PWT.

And we understand why. Where could be better than this lovely house, with its magnificent location looking down on the aching beauty of Portsalon Strand, as a place to recuperate, gather your thoughts, rejuvenate your senses, and just chill out, big time. Nowhere.

Croaghross offers salvation for body and soul, and the definitive cure for PWT, thanks to the utter professionalism of John and Kay Deane, and the elemental beauty of this peninsula. And the super food does its bit too: lamb marinated in orange and rosemary baked in puff pastry; cod with crème fraîche and cherry tomatoes; plaice stuffed with coriander and ginger; pear and walnut tart; gooseberry fool with baby meringues, not to mention one of the best breakfasts to be found in the country. There are lovely wines to choose from to help you get over that PWT. So don't despair: if you feel PWT coming on, simply act straight away, and get up to Portsalon.

- ● **OPEN:** 9 Mar-31 Oct
- ● **ROOMS:** Five rooms, all en suite
- ● **AVERAGE PRICE:** B&B £20-£35 per person sharing, £5 single supplement

- ● **NOTES:**
Dinner 7.30pm-8pm, £17.50, book before 10am
Vegetarian dinner with advance notice. Full Wheelchair Access. Private parking beside house. Children – welcome.
- ● Opposite the golf club, turn left at signpost.

10 ROMANTIC HOUSES

(1)

ASSOLAS COUNTRY HOUSE
CO CORK

(2)

BARNABROW COUNTRY HOUSE
CO CORK

(3)

BERRYHILL
CO KILKENNY

(4)

BROOK LODGE INN
CO WICKLOW

(5)

DOLPHIN BEACH
CO GALWAY

(6)

ECHO LODGE
CO LIMERICK

(7)

GLENALLY HOUSE
CO CORK

(8)

ISKEROON
CO KERRY

(9)

THE MILL RESTAURANT
CO DONEGAL

(10)

THE MOAT INN
NORTHERN IRELAND

THE GREEN GATE
Paul Chateanoud
Ardvally, Ardara, Co Donegal
Tel: (075) 41546

This collection of little cottages run by Paul Chateanoud won't appeal to those who need to be blown away by the water pressure in their showers, and who want trouser presses and isdn lines and enough toiletries to marinate an elephant. These folk will look at The Green Gate and the adjective 'Spartan' will fill their thoughts.

But if you seek an ascetic aesthetic, then the steep climb (and it is very steep; you don't need a 4x4 to get here, but it would help) up to the green gates may give your soul some space to breathe and your consciousness a chance to recover from the stresses of city life.

M. Chateanoud, a Parisian who once ran a bookshop devoted to music titles, has left the Green Gate as a collection of related outbuildings, some of which are thatched, all collected around the main cottage where he himself lives and where one takes breakfast. The combination of tactile nature (you are hunkered up beside the hill, with panoramic views opening up away to the sea) and the ruddy elementalism of the cottages is just right, though some good cotton sheets would be a bonus. The rooms are low, ageless, stone-floored, the furnishings simple old stoves and tables, electric heaters. It's nouveau pauvre, and many will hate it, but if you have an eye for a precise yet unflattering aesthetic, then it is here. In summer, breakfast is taken at the stone table in the garden, with Christopher the tame robin dancing attendance on the seat beside you, and a high morning moon gazing down from a cerulean sky. Bliss. In the village of Ardara, by the way, there is a smashing, authentic pub called The Beehive Bar. Look out for the draper's measure.

● **OPEN:** All year
● **ROOMS:** Four rooms, all en suite
● **AVERAGE PRICE:** B&B £20 per person sharing, £10 single supplement

● **NOTES:**
No Dinner. No Credit Cards.
Wheelchair Access. Private parking beside house
Children – welcome.
● A mile beyond Ardara, up the hill.

THE MILL RESTAURANT & ACCOMMODATION ❷

Susan & Derek Alcorn
Figart, Dunfanaghy, Co Donegal
Tel: (074) 36985 Fax: 36985

The Mill is a smashing new discovery. Susan and Derek Alcorn have opened a stylish restaurant with rooms where his cooking is extremely fine and her stewardship of the house and the restaurant is especially adroit and correct.

The house sits hard by New Lake as you head out of Dunfanaghy driving westwards, a captivatingly beautiful location with the sort of magically wild landscape that you will find only in far north Donegal. This is the place of which the travel writer H.V. Morton once wrote that the quality of light is such that, 'If any man with a sense of beauty were compelled to see it every day, it would unfit him for the practical business of life.' You see that light, made most brilliant at sunset, from the rooms upstairs at The Mill, and it never fails to astonish.

The scale of The Mill is extremely pleasing, something we might attribute to the fact that it was once both home and studio to the watercolourist Frank Eggington. It retains the feel of a private house, even though the restaurant is fairly substantial and there are six guest rooms.

The rooms are pleasingly styled and decorated, with excellent furniture and, for those feeling very stressed out, the most powerful power showers we have ever come across in Ireland.

Mr Alcorn cooks very well and takes care of all the details – the soda bread is very good indeed. He makes a fine terrine of smoked salmon and crab; and has smart modern notes such as brill with deep-fried oysters and a basil mash, or a wild mushroom and leek stroganoff with sage, though there are also great people pleasers, such as beef with shallots and Donegal lamb with sweet potatoes. Very promising.

● **OPEN:** Mar-Nov
● **ROOMS:** Six rooms, all en suite
● **AVERAGE PRICE:** B&B £25 per person sharing, £5 single supplement

● **NOTES**
Dinner Tue-Sat, £21-£25, Sun lunch £14.95
Wheelchair Access. Children – welcome
● Just outside Dunfanaghy on the road to Falcarragh, overlooking the New lake.

ROSSAOR HOUSE
Brian & Anne Harkin
Ballyliffin, Inishowen,
Co Donegal
Tel: (077) 76498 Fax: (077) 76498
rossaor@gofree.indigo.ie

There is a simple fact with which you cannot disagree about Rossaor: people are very comfortable here, in Brian and Ann Harkin's fine house.

You see it at breakfast in the conservatory in the morning – as they peer out at the stupendous view that lingers down and down to Ballyliffin strand – helping themselves to fresh juices and fresh fruits and organic yogurts and maybe asking for a bowl of porridge, trying to decide if this is the morning for the great big Irish breakfast, or maybe once again they will go for the excellent scrambled eggs with smoked salmon, or maybe try the grilled kippers. They are at peace with themselves, relaxed and content. Having a great time.

Of course, they are having a great time because the Harkins are such terrific hosts, and because of its type – that cosy, swaddling, Irish vernacular style of decoration allied with genuine hospitality – Rossaor is a benchmark B&B. People come back here time and again, year after year, a lot of them allegedly to play golf (or, perhaps more accurately, to play alleged golf). But one suspects that Rossaor is the real reason why they return, for who could tire of such generous hosts, and such alarmingly gorgeous scenery. Donegal is developing fast right now – too fast, for our tastes – and maybe doesn't have that long a time left when it will stay the well-kept secret that it has been for the last decade. So don't delay in getting up to Inishowen and to Rossaor, and getting some of that happy comfort into your bones.

- **OPEN:** All year except Christmas
- **ROOMS:** Four rooms, all en suite
- **AVERAGE PRICE:** £25 per person sharing, £5 single supplement

- **NOTES:**
No Dinner. Reservation advisable.
No Wheelchair Access. Private Parking
Children – welcome, high chair, cot, babysitting
- Five miles from Carndonagh on the Buncrana road.

ANGLESEA TOWN HOUSE
Helen Kirrane
63 Anglesea Road, Ballsbridge, Dublin 4
Tel: (01) 668 3877 Fax: 668 3461

People who discover Helen Kirrane's lovely Anglesea House thanks to the Bridgestone guides have a habit of writing to thank us for the recommendation.

'Anglesea House in Dublin serves unreal breakfasts, but we made the mistake of staying for three of them,' writes Tim, one of our American correspondents. No mistake, Tim. Don't feel guilty, just enjoy it.

What's to enjoy? Orange juice and grapefruit juice to begin. Then perhaps some of that marvellous compote of fruits, and perhaps a little stewed apple on the side. You might go for the yogurt with baked fruits, given the day that's in it.

Then a bowl of Anglesea baked cereal, though this morning it might have been their truly excellent porridge.

What's it to be for a main plate, then? Bacon, egg and sausage? How about some devilled kidneys – the Leopold Bloom breakfast, given that we are in Bloom's city. Or it might be a smoked salmon omelette today, what do you think? Mind you, the kedgeree looks tempting – the kedgeree always looks tempting, doesn't it?

Or perhaps some fresh fish: a sliver or two of plaice, maybe some fine sole, or a fillet of salmon trout to get the day well underway?

Then a little tart and cream and, finally, some profiteroles with chocolate. Lots of coffee, of course, lots and lots of coffee.

All that!? It couldn't be real, could it?

It could, it is. What we have just described was what was on offer one morning for breakfast in Anglesea Town House, a breakfast unlike any other. Extraordinary, gargantuan, unbelievable, but quite, quite real.

- **OPEN:** All year, except Christmas
- **ROOMS:** Seven rooms, all en suite
- **AVERAGE PRICE:** £50 per person sharing

- **NOTES:**
No Dinner (plenty of local restaurants)
Enclosed car parking. No Wheelchair Access
Children – welcome, cots, babysitting
- In Ballsbridge, cross the river and turn right into Anglesea Road. The house is signposted half-way up on the right.

THE CLARENCE ©
Bono, The Edge & Harry Crosbie
6-8 Wellington Quay, Dublin 2
Tel: (01) 670 9000 Fax: 670 7800
clarence@indigo.ie www.theclarence.ie

The Clarence is not as hip as it used to be, and thank heavens for that. The mantle of 'grooviest place in the city' has now crossed the river northside to lay itself on The Morrison, which means that Robert van Eerde and his team, with Anthony Ely installed in the kitchen, are now liberated from self-consciousness and can get on with providing some of the best service in the city.

The kind of thing they do well extends from the smallest details – 'Our stay was brought to a great close when the valet at the valet parking filled up our car to save us driving around looking for a petrol station,' a guest from the North wrote to us – to the largest, which is to say that the design of the hotel is so impeccable that the entire place just oozes comfort.

The secret of the design lies in the fact that it has eschewed temporary fashion in favour of classic design notes. The Lutyens chairs, the restrained colour palette with its use of neutral tones, the sense of spaciousness in the public rooms, the amusement of the many Guggi canvases, all create a feeling of immense well-being.

The fact that the food in The Tea Rooms is so fine – and that the breakfast is so carefully considered and executed: don't miss the treat that is their eggs Benedict – completes this oasis of good taste and good times.

Of course, The Clarence is expensive, and you need to think more than twice about spending this sort of money, but if you do choose it for a special treat, it will be money well spent.

● **OPEN:** All year
● **ROOMS:** Forty nine rooms, incl penthouse & suites
● **AVERAGE PRICE:** £210-£1,500 for standard to penthouse rooms (all rates per night)

● **NOTES:**
Tea Rooms restaurant open lunch (£17) & dinner (£36)
Full Wheelchair Access
Valet parking service (locked parking)
Children – welcome, high chair, cot, babysitting
● Overlooking the River Liffey, just at Grattan Bridge.

FITZWILLIAM PARK HOTEL
Mary Madden
5 Fitzwilliam Square, Dublin 2
Tel: (01) 662 8280 Fax: 662 8281
www.fitzpark.ie info@fitzpark.ie

Remember that feeling of waking on a spring or summer's morning, waking in a room on the fourth or fifth floor of a Parisian hotel, and walking to the window and pulling the curtains? Voila! There it lies before you, the beautiful skyline of one of the world's great cities. Is there anything else so romantic, so laced with potential and promise? It's a sight to revel in, to luxuriate in.

You can get something of the same feeling in The Fitzwilliam Park. Take a front room on the third or fourth floor. In the early morning in spring or summertime, climb out of that cosy bed, walk to the window and pull back the heavy curtains and Voila! There it is before you, the skyline of one of the world's great cities. Is there anything else so romantic, so laced with potential and promise? It's a sight to revel in, to luxuriate in.

Directly before you is the architectural perfection of Fitzwilliam Square, that jewel of Georgian architecture, and stretching away from it on all sides is dear old Dublin, setting itself to rights as the day begins. It is exhilarating. But virtually every detail of this fine house – okay, so it's called an hotel, but to be honest it feels more like a house – is just as charming. The service is superb, the style of the rooms very correct, the grandeur of the breakfast room imposing and satisfying. Obviously, the rooms at the front of the house on the top floors are the most desirable, but even those at the rere are very well thought through. It's a super address, which is presently a well-kept secret. It won't stay that way for long. By the way, don't confuse it with the Fitzwilliam Hotel, a modern hotel on St Stephen's Green.

- **OPEN:** All year
- **ROOMS:** Forty rooms, all en suite
- **AVERAGE PRICE:** £95-£170 per person sharing

- **NOTES:**
No dinner. Conference facilities
No Wheelchair Access
Overnight car parking for residents. Children – welcome
- In the city centre, between Baggot St and Leeson St.

THE HIBERNIAN HOTEL
Barry Wyse/PJ Daly
Eastmoreland Place, Ballsbridge, Dublin 4
Tel: (01) 668 7666 Fax: 660 2655
info@hibernianhotel.ie www.slh.com/hibernia

They seem to be able to manage the impossible in The Hibernian. They seem to be able to spin illusions from the second you walk through the door.

For a start, The Hib is an hotel that doesn't feel like an hotel at all. Hotels feel organised, slick, big, impersonal. But this hotel feels, instead, like a family home, where they just happen to take guests. It is a fine big building, but the arrangement of the entrance and the public rooms and the dining rooms is intimate and welcoming, like being in a grand house rather than a grand hotel.

The Hib also feels as if it is located in some little oasis of calm. You can stay here and be unawares that one of the busiest streets in Dublin is – literally – a mere stone's throw away. But the second you walk through the door, that feeling overtakes you: The Hib is a little republic of calm and dignity. To hell with the traffic and the noise: it simply vanishes.

And where the food in hotel dining rooms is usually to be avoided, the Hib created one of the first hotel dining rooms that was a destination restaurant in its own right, setting a precedent for places such as The Clarence and The Morrison. Norbert Neylon, the new executive chef, has a distinguished c.v. and promises exciting cooking.

To create this series of illusions is a mighty skill, but it comes as no surprise that manager David Butt should have created the very thing that makes The Hib special, for he is one of the finest hoteliers you can meet: genial, expert, genuine, a man able to motivate staff to create a place where they seem to be able to read your mind.

● **OPEN:** All year, except Christmas
● **ROOMS:** Forty rooms, all en suite
● **AVERAGE PRICE:** Single room £120, £150-£185 double occupancy

● **NOTES:**
Dinner 6.30pm-10pm, (7pm-9pm Sun, residents only)
Full Wheelchair Access. Off-street Parking
Children – welcome, high chair, cot
● Where Upper Baggot Street meets Pembroke Road.

THE MORGAN ©
Paddy Shevlin
10 Fleet Street, Dublin 2
Tel: (01) 679 3939 Fax: 679 3946
sales@themorgan.com
www.themorgan.com

The Morgan is the ultimate city hotel. It puts you right in the heart of the city, but manages to let you get right away from the city, just by walking through that door.
It's smack in the middle of Dublin's Temple Bar quarter, and yet, somehow, it manages to seem right out of it. Walking in through this discreet entrance (blink and you miss it!) is almost like entering a cave. You are aware of all the city's buzz, but you can enjoy it, or escape from it. The Morgan is utterly self-contained. It is a solipsist's heaven. The simple, subdued but stylish décor adds hugely to the sense of freedom. The everywhere-but-nowhere style of its internationalism is perfect for a hideaway. You could wake in the middle of the night – woken perhaps by a bleary street-level rendition of 'The Fields of Athenry', as we were last time – and wonder where on earth you are. But the comfort of the rooms means you wake refreshed. For this is not the blandness of the international hotel room. For a start, all the rooms are differently designed and decorated, this is a genuine boutique hotel, and for our money the newer rooms are the tops.
The alone-perfectly-alone atmosphere is accentuated by the fact that there are no public areas: breakfast is taken in your room, discreetly and efficiently delivered, served on stylish cutlery and crockery.
If you want the action and company of a standard hotel, The Morgan is not for you. But if you need to escape, then here is the place for that respite, that assignation.

● **OPEN:** All year, except Christmas
● **ROOMS:** Sixty one rooms, all en suite
● **AVERAGE PRICE:** from £130, £105 per night single

● **NOTES:**
No dinner. Room service menu.
Breakfast from £7
Full Wheelchair Access
No private parking (public car park across the street)
Children – welcome, high chair, cot
● In Temple Bar, across from the ESB shop.

THE MORRISON
Hugh O'Regan
Lower Ormond Quay, Dublin 1
Tel: (01) 887 2400 Fax: (01) 874 4039
info@morrisonhotel.ie www.morrisonhotel.ie

The great gift which fashion designer John Rocha has brought to The Morrison has been to bestow a tactility to the design from which the hotel benefits greatly. Even though the doors to the rooms are opened electronically, for example, they do give you a key, for they want to downplay the slickness of electronic sophistication.

You can describe it as a style temple, as many have done, but it succeeds because it manages to get beyond mere style into something more interesting.

The rooms are very earthy: granite sinks in the bathroom; the throw with its glinting ivory colours on the white bed; the low-lying dark wood furniture; the cinnamon sticks in the large glass bowl; the excellent towels and toiletries. The rooms at the front of the hotel are ace, with magnificent views over the River Liffey and these are always the ones to request.

Opinion on the public spaces in the hotel is more divided. Some find the colours too dark, the walkways too dimly lit, and if you don't like them, then no amount of style gurus will convince you otherwise.

The Halo restaurant, with its dramatic atrium construction, and the downstairs Lobo bar with its oriental theme and acres of white leather, blood red cushions and a fifteen foot African head, hand-carved by Eoin Byrne, are both very well considered. Of course, its reputation as a style temple means that it attracts a somewhat self-conscious crowd at times, but they don't detract from the fact that The Morrison is hugely enjoyable.

- **OPEN:** All year
- **ROOMS:** Forty rooms, all en suite
- **AVERAGE PRICE:** £175-£350 per room

- **NOTES:**
Restaurant serves breakfast, lunch (£25), dinner (£45)
Recommended for Vegetarians.
No Wheelchair Access. Off street Parking.
Children – welcome, but no dedicated menu.
Reservations essential.
- Overlooking the River Liffey.

NUMBER 31
Noel & Deirdre Comer
31 Leeson Close,
Dublin 2
Tel: (01) 676 5011 Fax: 676 2929
number31@iol.ie www.number31.ie

Who is the real boss of Number 31? Well, Noel and Deirdre Comer run this smashing house with great skill and hospitality – '# 31 – what a wonderful place!' wrote an American correspondent who discovered this little jewel thanks to a Bridgestone Guide, and that's no more than a typical response – but frankly, our money is on Homer Comer as the real master of this house.

Homer isn't a refugee from The Simpsons come to Ireland. In fact, he's the rather patrician dog who slowly ambles his way around the house, letting you know, in a quiet, rather patrician way, that whilst Noel and Deirdre do the meeting and greeting and cooking, in fact he's is the chap who rules the roost. Right on, Homer!

Number 31 is one of the true cult addresses. It's a curious house, inasmuch as one part of it – the mews – is an ultra-modern sort of duplex, with a huge central room with sunken seating which is pure 1960's classic design. But then the other part of the house is a classic Georgian terrace house, with massive rooms with massively high ceilings with massive windows. Nowhere else gives you such a choice: do you want to sleep in the style of the 18th or the 20th century? It's up to you.

And aside from the marvellous hospitality of Noel and Deirdre, what also makes Number 31 special is the sort of folks who stay here. They are always the most eclectic, unusual and interesting bunch you could imagine, and conversation soon sparks up around the breakfast table. '# 31 – what a wonderful place!' Too right.

● **OPEN:** All year
● **ROOMS:** Ten rooms, all en suite
● **AVERAGE PRICE:** B&B £60 per person sharing, £25 single supplement

● **NOTES:**
No Dinner (numerous local restaurants)
No Wheelchair Access. Locked Car Parking
Children – welcome. Recommended for Vegetarians
● Turn at Cooper's Restaurant onto Leeson Close.

SIMMONSTOWN HOUSE

James & Finola Curry
Sydenham Road, Ballsbridge, Dublin 4
Tel: (01) 660 7260 Fax: 660 7341
info@simmonstownhouse.com
www.simmonstownhouse.com

How do you make a house comfortable for guests? Well, in Simmonstown House, Finola Curry solves this age-old problem in this way: acute attention to the details of furnishings, paintings, housekeeping and cooking, and the ability to balance a finely understood aesthetic. Put this together and you achieve a house which is supremely comfortable, a house which succeeds in making you feel cared for precisely because it is so well cared for.

You can return to Simmonstown in the afternoon, worn out from work or shopping (or marathon running, as a group of Americans were when we last stayed) and the sense of serenity and peace in the house is sublime. Collapse into a sofa, sip some tea, admire the fine collection of paintings (which include a number of Markeys), and you really will have to work hard to find the will power to get up and get going once again. Few houses can manage such a sense of abandoned comfort, but Simmonstown achieves it in spades.

Mrs Curry makes a special feature of breakfast, served at the big four metre table, and it is a true treat: marinated prunes; great granola and muesli with yogurt; beautifully scrambled eggs with excellent bacon; tea from a silver tea pot, and sparkling silver service.

In summertime, the french doors are opened out, making the breakfast room even more attractive, whilst the seven rooms are all styled with care and circumspection: they feel just right. If you have to attend any manner of function in the RDS, then this address – right across the road from the main RDS building – is heaven-sent.

- **OPEN:** All year, except mid Dec-mid Jan
- **ROOMS:** Seven rooms, all en suite
- **AVERAGE PRICE:** B&B£50-£70 per person sharing

- **NOTES:**
No Dinner. Wheelchair Access. Enclosed Car Parking
Children – welcome
- Sydenham Road is a cul-de-sac off Merrion Road and directly opposite the RDS.

WATERLOO HOUSE

Evelyn Corcoran
Waterloo Road, Dublin 4
Tel: (01) 660 1888 Fax: 667 1955
waterloohouse@eircom.net
www.waterloohouse.ie

'It's just so special and nice to stay in a Georgian house,' said a friend from Edinburgh, who came to Dublin and stopped at Waterloo for a weekend and a few days, and was utterly charmed by the house.

It's a typical reaction, to tell you the truth.

'You should really put it in your book. They really looked after us,' was the response of some American friends who wound up here, and consequently wound up happy, and indeed it is just that aspect of looking after you that makes Waterloo different, and successful. Here is a house with the personal touch, seen in every aspect of the operation, and that quality makes Waterloo valuable, noteworthy.

It is a fine, tall Georgian building, set close to the Baggot Street end of Waterloo Road, which means that walking into town is a cinch, and yet the road is peaceful at night time, something that other houses in the city cannot always guarantee. The interior design is a blend of restrained business-like formality, and old-style plushness, and it has been well-judged and well-executed. The bedrooms are very comfortable and very intimate, and they suit both those who are in town on holiday and those who are in town on business.

Breakfast is taken downstairs in the small conservatory at the rere of the house, and again a lot of care is shown in its preparation and its service, by staff who are exceedingly helpful and friendly. A fine address.

● **OPEN:** All year, except Christmas
● **ROOMS:** Seventeen rooms, all en suite
● **AVERAGE PRICE:** B&B £35-£45 per person sharing, £65 single

● **NOTES:**
No Dinner
Wheelchair Access. Enclosed Car Parking
Children – welcome
● From the city, take the first right after Baggot Street Bridge, the house is on the left.

BALLYNAHINCH CASTLE HOTEL
Patrick O'Flaherty
Ballinafad, Recess, Connemara, Co Galway
Tel: (095) 31006 Fax: 31085
bhinch@iol.ie www.commerce.ie/ballynahinch

There are French bikers wrapped in expensive leathers walking in the door, meeting fishermen in lolloping waders who are heading down to the river. In the bar there are couples having a quiet drink and boisterous groups, locals and holidaymakers, romantic souls who fly upstairs from the dinner table even before their wine is finished, and lonely fishermen hoping to hook a friend for conversation in the bar, having failed to hook a fish.

Welcome to Ballynahinch Castle, a slice of the entire world brought to the wilds of Connemara.

The location of the castle is enchanting, and it is surrounded by gardens of impossible beauty (though there is rather too much rhododendron, we think). It's close to the main Galway-Clifden road, yet when you turn off the road at the canal bridge and make your way down to this series of loughs and lakes at the centre of which sits Ballynahinch, you enter another world.

This fairy-tale setting could be undermined by any shortcoming on the part of the staff, but service and cooking here are first class. Robert Webster has charge of the kitchens, and his cooking is polished and enjoyable: warm vegetable risotto with cherry tomatoes and balsamic; cheddar cheese soup with diced peppers; loin of rabbit with asparagus and chanterelles (why don't more chefs cook rabbit?); perhaps even, on a good day, a fish caught by a guest, which will be simply steamed and served with hollandaise and primavera vegetables. Service is charming, value for money is excellent, and the views from the window seats in the dining room are mighty.

- **OPEN:** Jan-Dec (closed Christmas week & Feb)
- **ROOMS:** Thirty-seven rooms, all en suite
- **AVERAGE PRICE:** B&B £52-£150 per person sharing, £20 single supplement

- **NOTES:** Dinner 7pm, from £23, tables always reserved for resident guests. Pub lunches.
No Wheelchair Access. Enclosed Car Park.
Children – price reductions
- Drive through Maam Cross and Recess. Turn left for Roundstone, and Ballynahinch is 4km down the road.

DEVON DELL
Martin & Berna Kelly
47 Devon Park, Lower Salthill, Galway
Tel: (091) 528306 Mobile (086) 3062185
devondell@iol.ie www.iol.ie/~devondel

'Details are attended to lovingly and thoughtfully,' an American visitor noted who stayed in Berna Kelly's much-admired house in Lower Salthill, just outside Galway city. God, of course, is in the detail, and Mrs Kelly knows that and understands it, and knows just how much it means to guests to have those details properly taken care of. In fact, it is simply impossible to feel comfortable in any house if the tiniest details are not regarded – for us, the death-knell of many a place to stay is actually the grouting: bad grouting, no Bridgestone.

Devon Dell is a newish house, so don't expect any period charm, but the rooms are big enough to be comfortable, and again it is in the details that Mrs Kelly wins out: excellent linens; exceptionally good breakfasts, with everything on offer from cereals and porridge or a compote of dried fruits with prunes and apricots; then a plate of fresh fruit with yogurt or cottage cheese; poached egg with potato waffles; smoked salmon with scrambled eggs; kippers on toast; the traditional fry-up; an apple and nut waffle with maple syrup; and a French toast special. When you arrive there is tea and scones, and the house has all the sort of magazines and books you never seem to manage to buy for yourself but are always happy to pore over when staying somewhere relaxing.

Galway has numerous places to stay, but finding a place in the city that is reliable and truly hospitable, and which doesn't just feel like someplace where they want to see your money and then see the back of you, is truly difficult. Devon Dell is just such a place.

- **OPEN:** 1 Feb-31 Oct
- **ROOMS:** Four rooms, all en suite
- **AVERAGE PRICE:** B&B £22.50 per person sharing. £25 single

- **NOTES:**
No Dinner. No Wheelchair Access. Car Parking
- On the Lower Salthill road, turn right at the orange painted shop (opp Devon Pk House). After 100m fork left, then left again into a cul-de-sac.

DOLPHIN BEACH ❷
Billy & Barbara Foyle
Lower Sky Road, Clifden
Co Galway
Tel: (095) 21204 Fax: 22935
dolphinbeach@iol.free.ie
www.connemara.net/dolphinbeach

What a lovely house this is, and what a location!
Billy and Barbara Foyle – and yes, they are members of
the Connemara Foyle family whose talented tentacles
extend to various places to stay in and around Clifden –
have converted and built a striking and yet very subtle
house which commands the most marvellous views down
to the beach – from where one can swim – and the sea
stretching out to the endless Atlantic.
It's tucked in between the Lower Sky Road and the sea,
and what is special about this area is the sense of space
which the vast expanse of sky contributes, and the ever-
changing light bouncing off the sea.
The Foyles have respected this light in planning the
house, and so the rooms – and the conservatory where
they serve breakfast and also run a small restaurant – is
beautifully washed with natural light: these are truly
charming, light-filled spaces, with an atmosphere
reminiscent of the Aegean, such is the power of the light.
The bedrooms are amongst the nicest new rooms we
have seen in a very long time, and, despite the lure of the
beach and the sand and the sun, it can be hard to
persuade yourself to get out of the room!
The Foyles and their girls are charming hosts, with just
the right note of informality to help you unwind and get
away from it all – and that is just what this splendid house
promises to allow you to do.

● **OPEN:** Mid Mar-mid Nov
● **ROOMS:** Eight rooms, all en suite
● **AVERAGE PRICE:** B&B £35-£45, £10 single
supplement

● **NOTES:**
Dinner Sun-Fri, 7.30pm, £23
Wheelchair Access
Enclosed Car Parking. Children – welcome
● Take the Sky road out of Clifden, take lower fork for
1 mile, it's the 1st house on the sea side.

ERRISEASK COUNTRY HOUSE HOTEL

Stefan & Christian Matz
Ballyconneely, Clifden,
Connemara, Co Galway
Tel: (095) 23553 Fax: 23639
erriseask@connemara.com
www.erriseask.connemara-ireland.com

It might be that the original reason why you come to Ballyconneely and to the Erriseask House Hotel is to sample the slice of culinary wonder that is Stefan Matz's acclaimed cooking. The nice surprise which will meet you, however, in addition to the expertise of the food, is the glorious, elemental location of this unusually designed and styled restaurant and hotel.

The hotel is pitched right beside the shore of Mannin Bay and its exposed setting is powerfully affecting: you seem to be right in the embrace of the elements here, the subtle yet strong colours, the endless skies with their curlicues of clouds, the ever-changing colours which so mesmerise visitors from the Mediterranean. It is a glorious spot, vitalising, energising.

Erriseask is really a restaurant with rooms – this is perhaps a more accurate description of the Erriseask complex which also boasts newish apartments with magnificent views out over the sea. These apartments are the most covetable of the rooms, though the original rooms have all been pleasingly improved over the years. The apartments make a great base for getting the most out of Connemara, and there is always the lure of Stefan Matz's sublime and bewitching cooking to look forward to, a chance to trade the embrace of the elements for the embrace of the ingredients.

- **OPEN:** End Mar-end Oct
- **ROOMS:** Thirteen rooms, all en suite
- **AVERAGE PRICE:** B&B £52-£65 per person sharing.

- **NOTES:**
Dinner 6.30pm-9pm
Limited Wheelchair Access. Enclosed Car Parking
Children – one family bedroom, high chair, cot
- From Clifden follow signs to Ballyconneely via the coast road.

FERMOYLE LODGE
Nicola & Jean-Pierre Stronach
Costello, Connemara, Co Galway
Tel: (091) 786111
www.fermoylelodge.com

'The place was really welcoming and the charm of the couple running it really won us all,' writes a friend who stayed at Nicola and Jean-Pierre Stronach's beautiful house, a handsome and resplendently remote hunting lodge built by the Berridge family in 1875.

Its remoteness is stunning: you drive from Oughterard for 11 miles (it can also be reached from the Spiddal road) along the windiest, wildest road you could think of. And there, amidst the rhododendrons, is this handsome lodge: it seems as if it can only have fallen from the sky. The remoteness accentuates the calmness of the house. The decorative style is restrained old decency, and perfectly done, with subtle hues of pinks and greys and creams. The dining room feels like something of a curiosity – one presumes it was added to the original house – but Jean-Pierre's cooking is the right sort of food: lightish French-influenced with a savvy knowledge of local ingredients and suppliers. He is a keen student of cooking, and it shows in suave and enjoyable food.

Two of the upstairs bedrooms have fabulous views out over Lough Fermoyle, and there are also two double rooms in a mews at the right side of the house, just as comfortable as the main quartet of rooms.

The water in Fermoyle is, as our friend noted, 'the colour of tea (Barry's not camomile!) I really enjoyed my bath and the chemistry of that brackish water is really very interesting, and good for them for leaving it as it is.' At certain times of the year, do note, midges can be a nuisance which will drive you indoors.

- **OPEN:** All year
- **ROOMS:** Four rooms, all with private bathroom
- **AVERAGE PRICE:** B&B £45 per person sharing, single supplement £15

- **NOTES:**
Dinner 8pm, £22
No Wheelchair Access. Unsuitable for young children.
- From Oughterard, turn left just before bridge & follow signs for Costello. Lodge is 11 miles further.

GARRAUNBAUN HOUSE
John & Catherine Finnegan
Moyard, Connemara, Co Galway
Tel: (095) 41649 Fax: 41649
garraunbaun.house@ireland.com

Handsome, serene, relaxing, poised, confident, charming. Not a bad raft of adjectives with which to describe a house, don't you think? But that is what we scribbled amidst our notes on a last visit to Garraunbaun in early summer. The house seems to us to be at its best at that time of the year. The light bouncing off the lakes and the impressive majesty of the Twelve Bens in the distance give a clarity to this staggering countryside of Connemara, and at such a time Garraunbaun feels like just the right place to be.

And Delia Finnegan is just the right woman to be running such a fine house. Each year there are small but significant changes, so the dining room has been newly relocated to what was the piano room – check out that lovely old Bluthner! – and it's a delightful place in which to enjoy Delia's cracking country cooking. 'I love the local wild salmon,' she will tell you. 'The fisherman came up the other day with four fish! So I freeze it when it's so fresh, to get the most out of the short season. And they bring me lobsters, and rock oysters and shrimp, and I have my own herbs.' She is thrilled with this palette of possibilities, but not as thrilled as you will be.

The house itself is quite lovely, and reminds us in many ways of another house featured in this book, Sea Court, near to Butlerstown in West Cork, run by David Elder, both charming, gracious and ultra-comfortable places to stay. This is one of the great addresses in the west. Oh, and don't miss out on Delia's apple juice.

● **OPEN:** All year
● **ROOMS:** Four rooms, all with private bathroom
● **AVERAGE PRICE:** B&B £35 per person,

● **NOTES:**
Dinner 8pm, separate or communal tables
No Wheelchair Access. Enclosed Car Parking
Children – high chair, cot, babysitting, video films
for all ages. No smoking
● Drive through Clifden, then Cleggan, then Westport, and you will find Garraunbaun's signs 3km further.

KILLEEN HOUSE
Catherine Doyle
Killeen, Bushypark Galway, Co Galway
Tel: (091) 524179 Fax: 528065
killeenhouse@ireland.com
www.killeenhousegalway.com

Time travellers ahoy!

If you want to step back in time and sleep back in time, then Catherine Doyle's fascinating and beautiful Killeen House is the place in which you will able to do it. Ms Doyle makes time travel a reality, and you don't need a Tardis or a space suit or anything else. Just bring yourself. It works like this: Catherine Doyle used to work in the antiques business, and has managed to furnish each room in different, meticulously sourced, design periods, with each piece of furnishing belonging to the correct period. The Art Deco room, for example, is a perfect piece of composition, with each element perfectly united in style and compatibility with every other piece. Sleep here, and you sleep back in time.

The effect in each of the suites – whether it be the Georgian, the Victorian, the Regency or the Edwardian – is to create rooms which have absolutely no discordant design notes whatsoever, which makes them wonderfully inviting, and wonderfully apposite. You feel you should be dressed in period costume, frankly.

The effect of this, however, is not to create a museum, but to create wonderful comfort. Many houses do not realise that the wrong object in the wrong place creates bad feng shui. Here, you see what happens when the right object from the right period is placed in the right place: the effect is to create calm, to create harmony. The public rooms are no less expertly detailed, and no less welcoming, and Ms Doyle has an aesthete's eye for every detail, including breakfast. So, if you hanker to leave the present behind, head to Killeen straightaway.

- **OPEN:** All year, except Christmas
- **ROOMS:** Five rooms, all en suite
- **AVERAGE PRICE:** B&B £40-£50 per person sharing, £20 single supplement

- **NOTES:**
No Dinner. No Wheelchair Access. Enclosed Car Parking Children – over 12 years welcome
- Bushypark is situated between Galway and Moycullen.

KILMURVEY HOUSE

Treasa & Bertie Joyce
Kilmurvey Bay, Inis Mór, Aran Islands, Co Galway
Tel: (099) 61218 Fax: (099) 61397
kilmurveyhouse@eircom.net
www. kilmurveyhouse.com

You will find it hard to believe, as you bask in the comfort of one of Kilmurvey House's twelve bedrooms, after an exhilarating and exhausting day spent swimming and walking and exploring on Aran, and after one of Treasa Joyce's delicious dinners, but Kilmurvey used to be the home of the 'Ferocious O'Flahertys'!

Add in the fact that the house is only twenty minutes by foot away from Dun Aengus, celebrated as the greatest 'barbaric Fort' in western Europe, and it all sounds as if Inis Mór is a tad too aggressive a place in which to take a holiday. Ferocious? Barbaric? What on earth is going on here?

Don't worry. Things have calmed down a bit since those days of ferocity and barbarity – though on a busy weekend in the summer Kilronan can be a pretty lively place – and the ferocity of the O'Flahertys has been replaced by the gentle, practised hospitality of Mrs Joyce. She is a meticulous housekeeper – 'everything gleams!' as a friend once breathlessly reported – and a fine cook. Breakfast and dinner are both a treat, good domestic cooking accomplished with panache and, vitally, just the sort of food to set you up for the day and to restore you at the end of a busy day exploring this fascinating island. Don't make the mistake, which many people do, and just come to Aran for an afternoon or a day. Come here and stay in Kilmurvey for a few days at least. It takes 24 hours for your time frame to shift to the steady-slow beat of the island, and when that happens is when you will enjoy Aran, and Kilmurvey, at their beautiful best.

● **OPEN:** 1 Apr-16 Oct
● **ROOMS:** Twelve rooms, all en suite (7 family rooms)
● **AVERAGE PRICE:** B&B £25 per person sharing, £35 single

● **NOTES:**
Dinner £16, 7pm, please book. Vegetarian meals with notice. No Wheelchair Access. Children – welcome
● 7km from the ferry port. Take a mini bus.

NORMAN VILLA
Dee & Mark Keogh
86 Lower Salthill, Galway, Co Galway
Tel: (091) 521131/521380 Fax: 521131
normanvilla@oceanfree.net

Of all the 100 places to stay featured in this book, Mark and Dee Keogh's Norman Villa is probably the most difficult house to actually get into.

Don't be deterred. Don't give up. You owe it to yourself to stay in (with?) Norman, to finally secure a room.

It's not big, of course, which doesn't help your chances. A mere five rooms, each and every one of them a little jewel of design nous, gorgeously tactile and complemented by exceptional housekeeping.

And Norman doesn't have customers, mere punters. Not a chance. It has devotees. The folk from the film festival book for next year when they are leaving this year. The theatre people are always here. The business set who couldn't tolerate the blandness of an hotel. Devotees, every one, people for whom it is simply unthinkable to stay anyplace else in Galway, so they make sure that booking into Norman is the first thing you do when planing any trip, any itinerary.

So, how to explain why these people should be so stubborn an obstacle in the way of your determination to enjoy Norman? Simple. Norman is just the coolest address, the most cult address, the hippest, hottest place to stay. It's a sublimely beautiful house, and Mark and Dee Keogh bring enormous chutzpah and vivacious energy to its endlessly pleasing space. They also have the most appreciative eye for furnishings and paintings – these guys could set out their stall tomorrow as interior designers and make a killing – and allied to their spontaneous hospitality, it makes Norman irresistible.

● **OPEN:** 1 Feb-30 Nov
● **ROOMS:** Six rooms, all en suite
● **AVERAGE PRICE:** B&B £37.50 per person sharing £45 single room

● **NOTES:**
No Dinner. No Wheelchair Access. Locked Car Parking
Children – over 6 years welcome. 25% discount.
No smoking in bedrooms. Vegetarians catered for
● The house is beside PJ Flaherty's pub in Lower Salthill.

SEAVIEW HOUSE
Sheila Griffin
Clifden
Connemara, Co Galway
Tel: (095) 21441
sgriffin@eircom.net

What a subtle, welcoming house this is. Sheila Griffin is a member of one of those great Connemara tribes who specialise in hospitality, for her brother is Hugh Griffin of the wonderful High Moors restaurant, just a mile outside of town (see the entry in the Bridgestone 100 Best Restaurants in Ireland guide).

Ms Griffin has the same sharp sense of humour as her brother, not least when she explains that Seaview is something of a oxymoron: the house no longer enjoys its sea view, as an apartment block has been built directly across the street, straight in line with her view of the harbour. No matter.

What is important is that Ms Griffin is as adept at hospitality as any of the Griffins, and that she creates a comfortable, noble house. Whilst we would be generally slow to recommend to anyone that they stay so close to the centre of Clifden – this town gets loud and raucous in the middle of the season – Seaview's location somewhat down the hill, getting away from the centre of town, means that it is peaceful, and inside it is furnished and decorated with imagination and care, with a demure bohemianism that we like a lot.

Good breakfasts and patient hospitality and help from Sheila are the final pieces in a quirky little jigsaw that has great charm and offers great comfort, not to mention fine value for money.

- **OPEN:** All year, except Christmas
- **ROOMS:** Six rooms, all en suite
- **AVERAGE PRICE:** B&B £25 per person sharing
£10 single supplement

- **NOTES:**
No Dinner. No Wheelchair Access.
Outside Car Parking
Children – no facilities
No smoking.
Home grown veg, fruits, and preserves.
- Right beside the Bank of Ireland.

QUAY HOUSE

Paddy & Julia Foyle
Beach Road, Clifden, Connemara, Co Galway
Tel: (095) 21369 Fax: 21608
thequay@iol.ie www.thequayhouse.com

'We light the fires because I hate to see a fire doing nothing and everyone loves the smell of turf.' So says Paddy Foyle.

Isn't that a wonderful idea: a fire doing nothing? What a typical Paddy Foyle thought. Here is a man who would perish at the idea of doing nothing, so restless and driven a character is he. Every year the inimitable Quay House sees change and changes, new ideas, new colours, new developments, as Mr Foyle keeps himself from doing nothing over the winter by embarking on more building and renovating and improving.

He doesn't need to do this. Quay House is and always has been one of the most gorgeous houses to stay in Ireland. Its style is unique, a design fetishists' dream, filled with interesting objects arranged with Mr Foyle's customary iconoclasm. Just trying to choose which room you would like to stay in is agonising, because every one is different and everyone is thrilling. Mind you, we suspect that like a lot of people it would be the Napoleon room which would be our first choice, its trio of huge windows looking out over the harbour, with Clifden arrayed away up the hill, close enough to stroll to, far enough away to give you a peaceful night. Paddy and Julia Foyle run this great house with patrician professionalism and a energy level which is remarkable. Breakfast in the conservatory is always a delight, and indeed that is what Quay House is: a delight, with its smell of turf, and those busy fires.

● **OPEN:** Mid Mar-end Oct
● **ROOMS:** Fourteen rooms, all en suite. Seven studios, with balconies and small fitted kitchens
● **AVERAGE PRICE:** B&B £40-£45 per person sharing, single occupancy £60. Enquire about special offers.

● **NOTES:**
No dinner. Wheelchair Access
Enclosed Car Parking by arrangement only
Children – welcome, high chair, cot
● Three minutes by car from Clifden town centre.

①

BUGGY'S GLENCAIRN INN
CO WATERFORD

②

THE CLARENCE
CO DUBLIN

③

DOLPHIN BEACH
CO GALWAY

④

GLENALLY HOUSE
CO CORK

⑤

THE MILL RESTAURANT
CO DONEGAL

⑥

THE MORGAN
CO DUBLIN

⑦

THE MORRISON
CO DUBLIN

⑧

NUMBER 31
CO DUBLIN

⑨

SHELBURNE LODGE
CO KERRY

⑩

SIMMONSTOWN HOUSE
CO DUBLIN

RADHARC AN CHLAIR
Mrs Bríd Poíl
Inis Oirr, Aran Islands, Co Galway
Tel: (099) 75019 Fax: 75019

Inis Oirr has a mystery about it, a sense of wonder and foreboding. We have written before that its strange elementalism, its simple isolation in the middle of the Atlantic, puts us in mind of the volcanic island where the disappearance takes place in Michelangelo Antonioni's astonishing movie, L'Avventura.

There is something about this place which is not easily understood or explained. You come here time and again, but can't seem to understand it any better. It's more than a little unsettling, to be honest: sea and sky can seem too threatening to be comfortable.

So, the comfort you need will have to be found in Bríd Poíl's lovely bungalow B&B, and be in no doubt that this will be the perfect shelter from your existential storm.

She is a fastidious woman, Mrs Poíl, a mainlander from County Clare, and she is justifiably proud of her work, of her house, of her hospitality, and above all of her cooking. It comes as no surprise to see, on her kitchen wall, certificates announcing that she has completed various cookery courses, most likely with merits and distinctions. She is a fine cook, and a good baker, so even the simplest cup of tea with a home-baked scone is a treat, whilst dinner is a fine feast of scrummy home cooking sharpened by the skill of someone who is not only proud of what they can do, but who clearly finds huge enjoyment in it.

Those who find Inis Mór too busy to conform to an ideal of Aran, or who find Inis Meain too insular and quiet (though neither is either one or the other) might find just the peace they seek in this perplexing paradise.

● **OPEN:** All year, except Christmas
● **ROOMS:** Six rooms, five en suite
● **AVERAGE PRICE:** B&B £16-£19 per person sharing, £22 single

● **NOTES:**
No Credit Cards accepted
Dinner 6.30pm, £14, separate tables
Bring Your Own Wine. No Wheelchair Access
Children – welcome. Irish spoken
● Peadar Poíl always meets visitors and gives you a lift up to the house (on his tractor).

ALLO'S TOWNHOUSE ©
Armel Whyte & Helen Mullane
41 Church Street
Listowel, Co Kerry
Tel: (068) 22880

If you had to name a couple who you could trust to create a dream townhouse, that couple might very well have been Helen Mullane and Armel Whyte.

The assured, sharp – and witty! – eye with furnishings and decoration which they revealed in the sublime Allo's Bar and Bistro gave some indication of the intelligence and good taste which this pair share. But few could have predicted that Allo's Townhouse would have been just as shockingly delightful as Armel and Helen have made it. This house is a masterpiece, as fine as anything created by the great hosts and housekeepers anywhere in Ireland.

The use of furnishings and objects is marvellously post-modern, with old objects used in an ironic, reflexive way – the multiple old mirrors in the bathrooms; the pedestal hoisted over the bathroom door in Room 1 – whilst the bedrooms luxuriate in a sensual sympathy thanks to cleverly chosen beds and the use of mirrors to magnify what is, in fact, quite a narrow old house.

The place is simply a definition of good taste – understated when it needs to be; comfortable when it needs to be; a house without a jot of self-conscious fashion-following. Allo's works because the style is always subservient to comfort, and yet at the same time the pleasure of that style is an integral part of that comfort. The aesthete rests easy here, where everything works to please the eye and the soul. The restaurant and the bar are just as beautiful as the rooms, and the combination of the three is simply, completely, magical.

- **OPEN:** All year
- **ROOMS:** Three rooms, all en suite
- **AVERAGE PRICE:** £90-£130 per room, single occupancy £60-£90

- **NOTES:**
Dinner and bar food served in Allo's Bar & Bistro.
No Wheelchair Access
Children – welcome
- Centre of Listowel, opposite the Garda station.

THE CAPTAIN'S HOUSE
Jim & Mary Milhench
The Mall, Dingle, Co Kerry
Tel: (066) 915 1531 Fax: 915 1079
captigh@eircom.net
http://homepage.eircom.net/~captigh

Jim Milhench was a seafarer before he met Mary, and they decided to crew together on the charming vessel which is The Captain's House. His nautical background explains how this landlocked place, right smack in the centre of Dingle – albeit with a garden dissected by a river – gets its name.

It is a rather small house, but Jim and Mary have designed the various rooms in such a way that the house has a lovely intimate atmosphere. Interestingly, it's the type of house where regular guests actually request the specific rooms which they most cherish. The favourite is Room 10, a lovely room with a sloping ceiling.

The scale of the rooms and the superb housekeeping make for a place which oozes comfort, and that comfort is then further congratulated by the splendour of the cooking and the baking – whatever you do, just don't pass on the porter cake, offered to all guests with tea when they arrive, for it is a rich, boozy, beautiful concoction, and the care taken with it is typical of just how Jim and Mary operate: attention to detail, everything properly rigged.

The couple's hard work and determination to do their best brings treats in for breakfast, such as fuchsia honey from Ballyferriter, alongside baked ham, local goat's cheese, Mary's own muesli, an array of peaches and prunes and mandarins, and their own marmalade, buffeted by bumper egg dishes and the traditional fried Irish breakfast. The Captain's is a friendly, fun house, with just the right spirit of shipshapeness and spit'n'polish to suit a bubbly town like Dingle.

● **OPEN:** Mar-Nov
● **ROOMS:** Eight rooms, all en suite, plus one suite
● **AVERAGE PRICE:** B&B £27.50-£30 per person sharing, £35 single

● **NOTES:**
No Dinner. No private parking
No Wheelchair Access. No Children
● Follow signs for Dingle town centre, Captain's House is 200m on the left after the roundabout.

HAWTHORN HOUSE
Noel & Mary O'Brien
Shelbourne Street, Kenmare, Co Kerry
Tel: (064) 41035 Fax: 41932
hawthorn@eircom.net

'When people arrive, they are coming into my home, and this makes it important for me,' says Mary O'Brien.

Mrs O'Brien comes from a family which ran the local Central Hotel for 25 years, and this deep background in the people business is immediately evident in her work. Hawthorn, for many years a beacon of hospitality in the cracking town of Kenmare, is a homey house, pleasingly simple, but vitally personable and welcoming.

Her greeting is true and vivid, and sets the tone of the house. You are here to have a good time – everyone who comes here seems firmly set on having a good time – and having a good time is what you will certainly do.

The bedrooms are pastel and pretty, small by comparison to some of the many purpose built B&B's around the town, but wholly appropriate for an old townhouse. They are not at all overdone, but are instead serene and amenable, quite feminine in style, and do note, young lovers, that there is even a honeymoon suite. The idea of a honeymoon in this sweet house in this sweet town is rather delectable, so go on, ask her.

Hawthorn House feels just the way a good B&B should, its nature and style set by the energy and capability of the owner, its comfort appropriately comforting for the traveller at the end of a long day touring the beautiful Kerry and Cork peninsulas, the breakfast ambience optimistic and promising, the intimacy of the house quickly making friends of all your fellow guests. It is fine value also, which completes the picture of a place and a town to fondly return to.

- **OPEN:** All year, except Christmas
- **ROOMS:** Eight rooms, all en-suite
- **AVERAGE PRICE:** B&B £20-£25 per person sharing £5 single supplement

- **NOTES:**
No Dinner (many restaurants locally)
Enclosed Car Parking. No Wheelchair Access
Children – welcome, babysitting arrangements made
- Between the two entrances to the Park Hotel.

ISKEROON

Geraldine & David Hare
Iskeroon, Bunavalla, Caherdaniel, Co Kerry
Tel: (066) 9475119 Fax: 9475488
info@iskeroon.com www.iskeroon.com

There are two things that make Iskeroon special.
Let's start with the first. To get to the house, you have to do that thing that you have always wanted to do: you have to drive your car across a beach. Thrills! Thrills! Action man! Wonder Woman!
The location of the house is simply incredible: it is right at the bottom of an enormously steep hill down which you take all the corkscrewing left turns until you eventually drive across a small, flinty, pebble beach, and there it lies. But if the location is nakedly elemental, the house is marvellously protected from the elements, and you look out at the wild sea from its serene comfort, wrapped up in this work of art made of bricks and mortar, and sheer style.
And that is the second thing that makes Iskeroon special. It is simply, utterly, gorgeous, an undeniable design icon, with the location to match its dreamy beauty.
It was built by the Earl of Dunraven in the 1930's, and in the hands of David and Geraldine Hare, it is fortunate to have a couple who appreciate its uniqueness.
The style has design lovers slack-jawed with joy, plundering their texts to try to fathom a house that mixes elements of Lutyens with echoes of New England style, and features of the Arts & Crafts movement, then takes all of these things and turns them into something quite special. We have never seen a house with so many diverse elements so successfully unified. In some ways, the house feels like a work of art, its colours so well expressed, its location adding to the feeling that you are captured in the midst of something which someone is painting.

● **OPEN:** In 2001 only (new baby!) 1 May-10 June, 1-30 Sept. Self catering available in June, July & Aug
● **ROOMS:** Three rooms, all with private bathrooms
● **AVERAGE PRICE:** B&B £38 per person sharing, £10 single supplement

● **NOTES:**
No Dinner. Wheelchair Access
Not suitable for children under 12 years
● Bear left at Bunavalla Pier, bear left at each bend.
Go through 'private' gate, cross beach and enter gates.

MILLTOWN HOUSE
Mark, Anne & Tara Kerry
Milltown, Dingle,
Co Kerry
Tel: (066) 915 1372 Fax: (066) 915 1075
milltown@indigo.ie http://indigo.ie/~milltown/

The Kerry family is now securely installed as the confident and capacious innkeepers of Milltown House, a handsome house dating from the 1850s, with the most brilliant location imaginable.

You head out of Dingle on the Ventry road, and, having crossed over the bridge you turn left, heading down to the water and the house itself. From the breakfast conservatory of Milltown, the views out across Dingle Bay are stunning, and yet the short distance from the town itself, which can be much too crowded and boisterous during the season, means that the house is calm, relaxing.

It is a big house, with ten guest rooms all told. The style mixes and matches but everything is appropriate for the period of the house: the public rooms are spacious and comfortable, with fires and easy chairs, and it might prove difficult, after a good breakfast of Ballyhea kippers, or honey pancakes with berries or Dingle black and white pudding with eggs, to persuade yourself to get far beyond the sitting room and a lazy book and a little snooze.

Cineastes might like to know that Robert Mitchum stayed in Milltown when David Lean was shooting his God-awful movie, Ryan's Daughter, and Bob's own room is now Room 2. The great film critic David Thomson has written of Mitchum's 'candid unhappiness marooned on the Dingle peninsula with David Lean's lush and slow Ryan's Daughter', but candid happiness is more likely to be your state of mind in Milltown House.

- **OPEN:** Early Feb-end Nov
- **ROOMS:** Ten rooms, all en suite
- **AVERAGE PRICE:** B&B £37.50-£47 per person sharing, single on request

- **NOTES:**
No evening meal.
1 room special needs friendly, full wheelchair access.
Children – not suitable for under 12s. Car parking.
- Leave Dingle on the Ventry road, left over bridge.

THE PARK HOTEL ©
Francis Brennan
Kenmare, Co Kerry
Tel: (064) 41200 Fax: 41402 phkenmare@iol.ie
www.parkkenmare.com

What is the Park Hotel really like?
It's like a beautiful actress, we think. Someone who gets older, and yet gets more interesting, gets more beautiful. If you know it well enough, you will understand that it's the Catherine Deneuve of hotels: every year, it is more stunning, more gracious, more captivating, more alluring, more elegant. Age cannot wither it. It is the aristocrat of hotels.

It's an imposing building, built at the end of the last century by Great Southern Railways, but not at all a forbidding place. The style is subtle, never overstated, and very comfortable. And if one needs to know how its magic is achieved, the answer is simple: Francis Brennan leads his team from the front, and his team follow him to the letter.

Or, in his case, they follow him in knowing the correct way to dress a bed and lay out towels and robes; the correct placement of a pen and paper; the correct number of utensils and crockery on an afternoon tea plate; the correct table placements for breakfast and dinner; the correct way to pour a glass of wine; the correct way to carry a drink to table.

The simple mechanics of service are raised to an art form by this dynamic but understated man, and it is this feature which has always made The Park both so comfortable, and yet so authoritative. To see service made so transcendent is a pleasure in itself, but to be able to enjoy it in these luxurious confines is not merely a pleasure, it is a privilege. Age cannot wither it, and it just gets better and better.

- **OPEN:** Apr-Nov
- **ROOMS:** Forty eight rooms, nine suites, all en suite
- **AVERAGE PRICE:** B&B £161 per person sharing, £168 single room price

- **NOTES:**
Dinner 7pm-9pm, £44. Vegetarian option always on menu. Car Parking. Wheelchair Access
Children – welcome, cots, high chair, baby listening, early dinner in room for toddlers
- At the top of the town in Kenmare.

SHEEN FALLS LODGE ©
Bent Hoyer
Sheen Falls Lodge, Kenmare, Co Kerry
Tel: (064) 41600 Fax: 41386
info@sheenfallslodge.ie www.sheenfallslodge.ie

The Sheen Falls Lodge is glossy, but not trashy.

That's just about one of the most difficult balancing acts to achieve in the hospitality business, but they manage to achieve it here, thanks to serene service and dedication to their task which is truly admirable.

The secret of their success is not just the luxuriousness of the hotel – though it is indeed luxurious, with capacious bedrooms with all manner of mod cons and with no expense spared in the public rooms. But what is of more importance is the fact that they understand that true luxury, and creating a feeling of true luxury, lies with creating truly responsive, genuine, service. The mod cons mean nothing if there is no human hand making sure you have everything you need.

The management of the hotel has always been nothing less than exemplary, with Adriaan Bartels currently proving that he is the equal of any hotel manager in Europe.

For many travellers, then, the Sheen Falls is the proverbial definition of luxury. 'If you asked me where I would want to go for a dream weekend, just the two of us getting away from the kids for a few days, then Sheen Falls is it', a woman told us once, and she wasn't the first to say it and nor will she be the last.

Certainly it is an expensive place to stay and eat, but the Falls is never overblown, never vulgar, and it is easy to understand how this fine hotel, close to the beautiful town of Kenmare, represents an ideal of luxury for so very many people.

● **OPEN:** 2 Feb-Oct
● **ROOMS:** Sixty one rooms
● **AVERAGE PRICE:** £180-£520 per room

● **NOTES:**
La Cascade Restaurant serves dinner, £42.50, lunch available in sun lounge. Vegetarian and special diets catered for. Full Wheelchair Access. Children – welcome, all facilities. William Petty Conference Centre, Health Spa, 300 acres with fishing, horses, clay pigeon shooting
● Signposted as you enter Kenmare from Glengariff.

SHELBURNE LODGE
Tom & Maura Foley O'Connell
Killowen, Cork Road, Kenmare, Co Kerry
Tel: (064) 41013 Fax: 42135

Not only was Shelburne Lodge the most stylish house they stayed at during their holiday, some friends advised us, but it also served what was the best breakfast they ate anywhere: 'Maura's shimmering jewel-pink poached peaches were to die for!' they exulted, and added, 'and so was everything else!'

That's what Shelburne, Maura and Tom Foley-O'Connell's gorgeous house, just on the Cork road on the edge of Kenmare town, does to people. It is an icon address in every way: the design is so singular and so successful that it fair takes your breath away, the choice and arrangement of furnishings, paintings, and, in the bathrooms, the mirrors, is so stylishly achieved that it creates not just a feeling of well-being the minute you walk in the door, but a feeling of utter sumptuousness, a feeling completed by the breakfasts, which are superlative.

Yet it is not an indulgent sumptuousness – Mrs Foley is too disciplined just to hang swags and bows everywhere, or to have thrown money at the house indiscriminately. Simply to talk to her about the sources from which she culled the interior pieces is fascinating, because one realises what sheer hard work went into creating this vision of perfection. She is a woman of great taste and discernment, virtues shown both in her design sense and in her cooking: for here is a cook who makes the commonplace foods seem exotic, thanks to her quiet skill, and the Shelburne breakfasts are amongst the very best. You come away from this magical house feeling inspired.

- **OPEN:** 1 Apr-30 Oct
- **ROOMS:** Seven rooms, all en suite
- **AVERAGE PRICE:** B&B from £45 per person sharing, £15 single supplement

- **NOTES:**
No Dinner (good restaurants locally)
Enclosed Car Parking. No Wheelchair Access
Children – welcome, high chair, cot
- 300m from Kenmare, across from the golf course on the Cork road.

TONLEGEE HOUSE
Marjorie Molloy
Athy, Co Kildare
Tel: (0507) 31473 Fax: 31473
tonlegeehouse@eircom.net
http://homepage.eircom.net/~tonlegee

One can have nothing but the most profound admiration for Marjorie Molloy, and for the astonishing strength of character she has shown in continuing to run Tonlegee House, following the too-early death of her husband and partner, Mark.

For a decade, Tonlegee was their labour of love, and together they created a singular, special house where Mr Molly's cookery proved itself to be the best cooking for many miles around.

Mrs Molloy continues that tradition of genuine, true, considerate hospitality, allied to good cooking, today, whilst still managing to rear her young family. Like all the most talented people in the hospitality business, the energy of the house comes from her redoubtable spirit, and her defiance to the sheer challenge of her circumstances. Everything one expects of Tonlegee remains as reliable and steadfast as ever: the comfortable rooms with their aptly judged style are always welcoming, whilst the lounge where one chooses from the menu whilst taking an apéritif always pleases. Then there is the pleasure of a fine dinner of properly cooked modern country food in the softly lit dining room where locals and visitors enjoy dinner: a baked crab and ginger parcel with yogurt and soya; quail and wild mushroom pie with madeira; shredded duck confit with potato galette; rack of lamb with a gratin of white turnip. Breakfasts are particularly good, especially the marvellous scrambled eggs with chives.

● **OPEN:** All year except two weeks in late autumn
● **ROOMS:** Twelve rooms, all en suite
● **AVERAGE PRICE:** B&B £40 per person sharing, £10 single supplement

● **NOTES:**
Dinner Mon-Sat, £25-£30
No Wheelchair Access. Children – welcome
● Leave Athy by crossing over Barrow Bridge and Canal Bridge. You will see the Tegral factory on your left, then take the next left where the house is signposted.

BERRYHILL

George & Belinda Dyer
Berryhill, Inistioge, Co Kilkenny
Tel: (056) 58434 Fax: 58434
www.berryhouse.com info@berryhillhouse.com

If you didn't have the sharp, self-deprecating sense of humour which Belinda Dyer has, then a frolicsome, storybook house like Berryhill, sitting on the hill looking down on the storybook village of Inistioge, could threaten an experience that was rather twee, rather suffocating.

When you tell people, for example, that the three rooms in Berryhill have animal themes, and that one is decorated with piggies, one with frogs, and one with elephants, they look at you closely, to see if, like Liam Lawlor, you have simply lost the run of yourself, and have entered that state of solipsistic delusion which means you cannot separate what is real from what is unreal, or at least what is real from what is surreal.

But if Berryhill sounds bizarre, rest assured that the good, rich humour of the Dyers rescues it from being twee or suffocating, and indeed their humour makes it a smashing, fun house. The rooms do indeed have collections of figures which pay tribute to pigs, elephants and frogs, but it is all so ironically and amusingly done that you wonder why everyone doesn't do it.

Aside from the animal figurines, the rooms are exceptionally comfortable and, as we have remarked before, the elephant room does have the added bonus of allowing one to take a bath by firelight, an experience to be savoured and never forgotten.

The cooking at breakfast is excellent, and the public rooms are grand, sociable places in which to linger for longer than you had ever intended. A simply lovely house.

● **OPEN:** 1 May-31 Oct
● **ROOMS:** Three double suites (one is a family room)
● **AVERAGE PRICE:** B&B £45 per person sharing
£10 single supplement

● **NOTES:**
No Dinner – three local restaurant menus to peruse
No Wheelchair Access. Enclosed car parking
Children – over eight years welcome.
● From Inistioge, cross the bridge, bearing right, take the next left, then right and the house is the 2nd on the left.

IVYLEIGH HOUSE
Dinah & Jerry Campion
Bank Place, Portlaoise, Co Laois
Tel: (0502) 22081 Fax: (0502) 63343
ivyleigh@gofree.indigo.ie
www.ivyleigh.com

'I love cooking,' says Dinah Campion. 'I just love food,' she adds, before explaining that she takes classes each year with local cookery teacher Blanaid Bergin – 'to get new ideas, learn new dishes' – and has also had classes with Eugene MacSweeney, formerly of Kilkenny's Lacken House.

This gives a potent clue to Mrs Campion's character; she is driven by the desire to do the very best she can, and applies this to each detail of Ivyleigh House.

'I cook everything fresh,' she says. 'A fried breakfast must be cooked from the pan. And with baking you must use butter and cream. And if you make tea, you must use leaf tea.' And this searching for perfection is found also in the housekeeping in Ivyleigh, housekeeping which is of a stratospheric standard, with every room finished and polished to a dazzling, glistening conclusion. It's no surprise, then, that her bedlinen comes from Bottom Drawer in Brown Thomas, that her crockery is Mason's Chartreuse, that the house has an unusual Chippendale bow-end bed in one room, that the porridge she uses is Macroom Oatmeal, even that she has managed to find a way to repair sash windows which works.

There are five rooms, with the yellow room at the front of the house a particular favourite. Downstairs, the public rooms are capacious and grand, and breakfast begins with a buffet before moving on to carefully sourced foods: Clonakilty puddings; Superquin sausages; bacon from local man Noel Delaney; Cais Ban cheese as a vegetarian alternative; and Mrs Campion's Cashel Blue cheesecakes.

● **OPEN:** All year
● **ROOMS:** Four rooms, all en suite
● **AVERAGE PRICE:** B&B £36 per person sharing
£10 single supplement

● **NOTES:**
No Dinner. No Wheelchair Access. On street
car parking. Children – over eight years welcome.
● In the centre of town.

PRESTON HOUSE
Allison & Michael Dowling
Main Street, Abbeyleix, Co Laois
Tel: (0502) 31432 Fax: 31432

What do men and women want?
Everything.
Know anyone who can do that for us?
Allison Dowling.
For travellers on the N7, Mrs Dowling offers a refuge in
Preston House, in the gorgeous village of Abbeyleix. She
gives us smashing comfort in the four bedrooms above
the restaurant, clever and comfortable rooms, designed
and decorated with a precise vision. Just what we want.
And then Mrs Dowling completes the performance by
offering us exactly the sort of comfort food we want
when we seek refuge from the road, food to soothe the
soul, whilst salving the stomach.
She bakes good breads and scones to start, and cooks
very classical starters: grilled goat's cheese with red onion
chutney; smoked salmon on brown bread; deeply
flavourful cream of vegetable soup. The meats of County
Laois are put to excellent use: sirloin with green
peppercorn sauce and mushrooms; loin of venison with
redcurrants, and there is good local duckling with plum
and port sauce, sautéed chicken with tagliatelle, light
cheese soufflé with salad, and the classics of the dessert
menu: crème brûlée; ice creams with meringues; raspberry
and almond torte.
She spoils us, does Allison. She knows exactly what we
want and she knows exactly how to make sure we get it.
That is her gift of hospitality, and the vivacious welcome of
Preston House is always summoning us to pull off the
road and knock on that handsome door.

- **OPEN:** All year (except 10 days at Christmas)
- **ROOMS:** Four rooms, all en suite
- **AVERAGE PRICE:** B&B £26 per person sharing
£5 single supplement

- **NOTES:**
Cafe open lunch and dinner. Reservations always helpful,
Advise Allison on your requirements when booking.
Wheelchair Access. No smoking in bedrooms.
Children – welcome, high chair, cot
- On the main street in Abbeyleix (the Dublin/Cork road).

ROUNDWOOD HOUSE
Frank & Rosemary Kennan
Mountrath, Co Laois
Tel: (0502) 32120
Fax: 32711
roundwood@eircom.net
www.hidden-ireland.com/roundwood

Cast a cold eye on Roundwood, Frank and Rosemary Kennan's house, and you might notice the elusive grouting in the bathrooms, the Heath Robinson-ish plumbing, the air of ramshackle and wear and tear in the public rooms downstairs.

For here is a Palladian house which does not tend or pretend to be pristine. It is an ordinary house, an old, handsome but ordinary house, which just happens to be old and rather lovely, and as such it is lovely to stay here. It works because it casts a spell on you.

And if its spell might seem unreal, it is all true. The ducks asleep on the lawn, the caw-caw of the crows, the cockadoodle-doo first thing in the morning, the cows under the tree, the true tastes of the cooking, the friendliness. It can be hard to leave Roundwood, hard to bid farewell to a place with such an ability to define what is special about Ireland.

Part of the pleasure is the confidently delicious, and quietly explorative, cookin of Mrs Kennan. She really does know how to cook the foods that suit us – and the serene dining room with its communal table – to a T: baked pears with a cream sauce; carrot and mint soup; stuffed lamb with roast potatoes and Piedmontese peppers, cassata – Roundwood is a house which can cast a spell on you.

● **OPEN:** All year except Christmas Day
● **ROOMS:** Ten rooms, all with private bathrooms
● **AVERAGE PRICE:** B&B £47.25 per person sharing £11.81 single supplement

● **NOTES:**
Dinner 8.30pm, £27.56, communal table. Book by noon. No Wheelchair Access
Vegetarians catered for
Children – welcome, high chair, cot, babysitting
● Turn right at T-junction in Mountrath for Ballyfin, then left onto R440. Travel for 5km on the R440.

HOLLYWELL COUNTRY HOUSE
Rosaleen & Tom Maher
Liberty Hill
Carrick-on-Shannon, Co Leitrim
Tel: (078) 21124 Fax: 21124
hollywell@esat.biz.com

Tom and Rosaleen Maher manage a great house, a place of consummate hospitality and charm.

Hollywell sits on the hill just outside of Carrick-on-Shannon, and from the dining room you feel you could toss a stone into the Shannon. This room is at its best at breakfast time, when the view from the windows creates an impressionistic painting of the beauties of this area; gentle colours that are more restrained than you find around the coast, the glint of light off the river stirring the room awake, subtle beauty.

The Maher's have mighty energy, and great senses of humour as well as great senses of hospitality. In fact, it's possible to stay here and to convince yourself that the other guests must surely all be family members staying with the Mahers for a few days. I mean, no one who wasn't family could possibly be that relaxed, could they?

The answer is: yes they could and yes they are. You won't find people being just as chilled out in many places as you find here.

Breakfasts are served in the main room around the grand piano, and they are deft and delicious, with every ingredient very well sourced and judged. The two front rooms have lovely views over the river, and if you can secure one of these, they should be your first choice, though the other rooms are all comfortable and inviting. By the way, if setting off for a day's boating or touring, don't forget to assemble your picnic at Trevor Irvine's shop, Cheese Etc., on Bridge Street in the town.

- **OPEN:** 2 Jan-20 Dec
- **ROOMS:** Four rooms, all en suite
- **AVERAGE PRICE:** B&B £35 per person sharing, £5-£10 single supplement

- **NOTES:**
No Dinner. Enclosed Car Park. No Wheelchair Access Children over 12 years welcome
- From Carrick-on-Shannon, cross the bridge, keep left at Gings Pub. The entrance to Hollywell is on the left.

BALLYTEIGUE HOUSE

Margaret & Dick Johnson
Rockhill, Bruree, nr Charleville, Co Limerick
Tel: (063) 90575 Fax: 90575
ballyteigue@eircom.net
http://homepage.eircom.ie//~ballyteigue

'We do not intend to expand and are happy the way we can manage. We try to keep what we have in good shape and improve where necessary.'

Every bed and breakfast keeper in the country should have these words of Margaret Johnson inscribed, if not on their hearts, then at least above the doors of their houses. How wise, how modest a sentiment they represent, and how indicative of the sanguine good sense which dominates the good house that Mrs Johnson runs, right here on the border between Limerick and Cork.

Ballyteigue is handsome, and superlatively comfortable, and immaculately managed. If you had just flown the Atlantic, picked up a car from Shannon and headed south, and Ballyteigue was your first port of call to have dinner and sleep the good sleep, then you would be starting off with one of the best examples of what Irish hospitality, and good Irish domestic cooking, is all about.

Here, in an unfussy, unshowy way, with plenty of attention to detail, you would find true-flavoured food, cooked by Mrs Johnson, cooking which once caused a correspondent to affix two exclamation marks to his letter to describe his delight 'What meals!!'.

He might have added 'What hospitality!!', or 'What comfort!!'. Mrs Johnson knows exactly what she can do, and the best way to do it as well as she can, and that is why Ballyteigue House provokes the superlatives.

● **OPEN:** All year, except Christmas. Booking essential off season.
● **ROOMS:** Five rooms, four en suite, one single room with private bathroom
● **AVERAGE PRICE:** B&B £26 per person

● **NOTES:**
Dinner 7pm, £20, set menu, by arrangement only
No Wheelchair Access. Children – welcome. No smoking
● 2km off the N20, and signposted from the main road. Take first right after O'Rourke's Cross, driving south. Pass Rockhill on right and watch for the sign.

THE MUSTARD SEED
AT ECHO LODGE

Daniel F. Mullane
Ballingarry, Co Limerick
Tel: (069) 68508 Fax: 68511
mustard@indigo.ie

When we stay in a house, we are always looking for something simple which will help us try to describe just why we have included the house in this book of the best places to stay. In Dan Mullane's Echo Lodge, we found the answer in... the fruit bowl.

Some houses and hotels put a great, big, pile-it-high bowl of fruit in your room, apples and tangerines and grapes and kiwi fruit and whatnot, with perhaps even a ribbon to hold it all in place. Fine. Nice. But overdone.

In Echo Lodge, the fruit bowl was a small silver salver, and on it were two, perfectly ripe, fresh figs. Dan Mullane had not done 'the fruit bowl'. Instead, with the minimum of ingredients, and the maximum of consideration, he had created and composed what was, in effect, a living still life. He had, in his unique way, aestheticised the fruit bowl. For others, it's a cliché. For Mullane, it is a challenge.

There isn't a single thing in the beautiful Echo Lodge which his touch does not aestheticise, which means this is one of the finest places to stay and eat in the entire country. Mullane makes it look easy, as all the great masters of hospitality do, but just watch how his staff echo his every action (Echo Lodge is well named), just look at how he creates menus with Eoghan Sherry, the chef, which give you perfectly delicious, arousing food.

Just look at how each room has been considered as an individual entity, and how Mullane's acute eye considers and composes the furnishings and the paintings until everything is just right. The pleasures to be enjoyed from this man's appreciation of design are intense, and he is one of the great figures in Irish hospitality.

- ● **OPEN:** Mar-Jan, except Christmas
- ● **ROOMS:** Twelve rooms, all en suite
- ● **AVERAGE PRICE:** B&B £65-£100 per person sharing

- ● **NOTES:**
Dinner 7pm-9.45pm, £34
Full Wheelchair Access. Children welcome, high chair, cot
- ● Take the Killarney road from Adare for a quarter mile. Turn first left (R519). Follow signs to Ballingarry.

10 GREAT WEBSITES

(1)

www.adelesrestaurant.com
ADELE'S, CO CORK

(2)

www.barnabrowhouse.com
BARNABROW HOUSE, CO CORK

(3)

www.bridgestoneguides.com
BRIDESTONE GUIDES WEBSITE

(4)

www.lismore.com
BUGGY'S GLENCAIRN INN, CO WATERFORD

(5)

www.theclarence.ie
THE CLARENCE HOTEL, DUBLIN

(6)

www.croaghross.com
CROAGHROSS, CO DONEGAL

(7)

www.lordbagenal.com
LORD BAGENAL INN, CO CARLOW

(8)

www.megabytes.ie
BRIDGESTONE GUIDE NEWSLETTER

(9)

www.themorgan.com
THE MORGAN, DUBLIN

(10)

www.morrisonhotel.ie
THE MORRISON, DUBLIN

REENS FARMHOUSE
Tilly Curtin
Ardagh, Co Limerick
Tel: (069) 64276

Tilly Curtin belongs to that school of devoted and talented B&B keepers who are as dotey and delightful as a storybook granny. Surrender yourself into her care and your cares vanish amidst the pristine housekeeping and voluble friendliness of Reens farmhouse.

Seen from the road, the house looks rather dramatic and imposing, with a long straight driveway lined by trees culminating in a fine, stone house, with a grand conservatory wrapping itself around the entrance.

But, once inside, any element of hauteur is dispensed, as Mrs Curtin takes you into her care and brews some tea and, next morning, makes a cracking fry-up.

We first heard of the house when, locally, we encountered a gaggle of Americans on holiday. When we asked them where they were staying, we misheard their reply as, 'Silly Curtains'.

'Oh yeah,' we said, 'we know that sort of house. Leopard skin duvet covers as well, eh? Poor old you.'

'Not poor old us,' they said: 'Tilly Curtin's house is great. Reens Farmhouse. It's great.'

'Tilly Curtin's,' we said. And we blushed, and off we went to Reens. And the Americans were right.

There are no silly curtains in Tilly Curtin's. Reens is, like the other cuddly-granny B&Bs you will find in this book, almost a definition of spontaneous, genuine, charming Irish hospitality. The style of the house is a pure spit 'n' polish Irish vernacular, and it is all too easy to linger over breakfast around the great big table, as you chat with the other guests, and discuss the state of the world.

- ● **OPEN:** 15 Apr-30 Sept
- ● **ROOMS:** Four rooms, two en suite
- ● **AVERAGE PRICE:** B&B £25 per person sharing, £7 single supplement

- ● **NOTES:**
No Dinner
No Wheelchair Access
Children – welcome, high chair, cot, baby monitor
- ● Situated on the N21, the main Limerick to Killarney road. Do not go into Ardagh.

GHAN HOUSE
Paul Carroll
Carlingford, Co Louth
Tel: (042) 937 3682 Fax: 937 3772
ghanhouse@eircon.net www.ghanhouse.com

Carlingford has become the Monte Carlo of the North East in recent years, as this lovingly preserved medieval village has collated together a talented bunch of chefs and inn keepers, virtually all of whom are good, and all of whom are conscious of their good fortune in having been neglected by the mainstream tourist industry for many years. The nearby village of Omeath has been ruined by bad tourism, and its fate has given Carlingford a very clear idea of what it has, and what it wants to be.

And now, the time for the town has come, and Carlingford at the weekend buzzes with folk from Belfast and Dublin, hell bent on getting away from it all for the weekend, happily messing about on boats or maybe just enjoying the restaurants and pubs of the village and relaxing.

The Carroll family's Ghan House is an apt metaphor for the village. An eighteenth century house just a stone's throw from the village walls, the family have restored it aptly in recent years – last year adding eight new rooms which have retained the style of the main house – and they have created not just a fine house in which to stay, but also a good restaurant which showcases the impressive culinary skills of Joyce Carroll and her team. There is even a cookery school which features guest chefs. For their pains, the Carrolls have been rewarded with apt success – most weekends the house is full, and small groups find it perfect for small, mid-week conferences. The family are perspicacious and painstaking, and the quality of food and the good wine list reflect their determination to do their very best at all times.

- **OPEN:** All year (except 23 Dec-10 Jan)
- **ROOMS:** Twelve rooms, all en suite
- **AVERAGE PRICE:** B&B £37.50-£47.50 per person sharing, £30 single room, £45-£50 single in double room

- **NOTES:**
Residents Dinner Wed-Sat, (non-res Fri & Sat) £23.50-£26. Children – telephone for details.
No Wheelchair Access. Cookery School
- 3yrds beyond the town sign, coming from Dundalk.

NEWPORT HOUSE ©
Kieran & Thelma Thompson
Newport, Co Mayo
Tel: (098) 41222 Fax: 41613 KJT1@anu.ie

The impeccably patrician nature of Kieran and Thelma Thompson's formidable house blesses this redoubtable place with a grandeur, a magnificence, that few other Irish country houses can match. Newport is singular, aristocratic, comfortable in its skin, as the French – who love this house – might very well say.

Ceilings vault. Staircases cascade. Silences ascend. It is a Merchant-Ivory period drama come to life. Nowhere but Newport House engenders these feelings, nowhere else is like this anachronism set fast in the modern world.

But one feature of Newport which deserves special attention is the wholly expert nature of the food served here, a lot of which originates in their own garden.

Kieran Thompson describes the culinary philosophy of Newport as 'allowing the quality of the food to come out', and John Gavan, who has been cooking here for many years now, manages to do just that. This is very classical cooking, and the judgement of the chef and the formal manner of the service are the most sublime complement to this lovely house: sirloin with red wine butter; quail stuffed with a mousseline of chicken with a wild mushroom sauce; wild salmon en croute with a lemon and chive cream sauce; turbot with creamed leeks and champagne sauce. Mr Gavan delivers the food with precision, and whatever you do, don't miss their superb smoked salmon.

If you want the true country house experience, in all its mad grandeur, then you simply cannot do better than Newport. Others offer what is, in effect, a facsimile of the country house experience. Newport is the real thing.

● **OPEN:** 19 Mar-7 Oct
● **ROOMS:** Eighteen rooms, seventeen en suite
● **AVERAGE PRICE:** B&B £69-£86 per person sharing, single supplement £18

● **NOTES:**
Dinner 7pm-9.30pm, £34
Limited Wheelchair Access
Children – welcome, high chair, cot, babysitting
● In the village of Newport.

BOLTOWN HOUSE
Susan & Jean Wilson
Kells, Co Meath
Tel: (046) 43605

Susan Wilson is a gifted cook, as this winter dinner from Boltown House will make clear. To begin, a ramekin with smoked haddock, shrimps and potato baked en cocotte, with a slender cheese crust. Then, a very delicious bowl of chicken and watercress soup – 'essentially chicken stock with celery and watercress and a little sour cream'. Fillet of pork has been flattened out and cooked with cumin and coriander, and is served with caramelised apples, with a cream sauce sharpened by balsamic vinegar. There is beautiful Swiss chard from the garden, a gratin of leeks, and floury boiled potatoes. For dessert, a light-as-a-feather lemon soufflé. But dinner isn't even over yet, for there is a final cheese course with farmhouse cheeses in superb condition, bought from Sheridan's Cheesemongers.

This is super food, and it's no surprise that Boltown has been making a name for itself as both a great place to stay and a great place to eat. Ms Wilson learnt her trade with Catherine Healy, late of Dunderry Lodge, a restaurant whose food has achieved legendary status. The same exactitude which Catherine Healy could command seen in Ms Wilson's food, though it is by nature simpler, more suitable to this grand old house.

Ms Wilson runs Boltown with her mother, Jean. The house dates from 1740, and features an unusual split landing. The dining room is papered dark red and suffused with candle light for dinner, whilst one can have a stiff drink beforehand in front of a roaring fire in the sitting room. There are three rooms, two en suite and the third with its own bathroom, all authentic and welcoming.

- **OPEN:** All year, except Christmas
- **ROOMS:** Three rooms, two en suite
- **AVERAGE PRICE:** B&B £35 per person sharing, single supplement £18

- **NOTES:**
Dinner around 8pm, £24. No Wheelchair Access. Advance booking essential. Children – welcome
- From Kells take Oldcastle road for 4 miles, take second left (Kilskyre) after petrol station.

THE OLD WORKHOUSE
Niamh Colgan
Ballinlough, Dunshaughlin, Co Meath
Tel: (01) 825 9251 Fax: 825 9251
comfort@a-vip.com http/travel.to/oldworkhouse

Why is Niamh Colgan's Old Workhouse so comfortable? Well, just take a look at those mattresses, for a start. Look at them! A foot deep in thickness, every one of them. Imagine the blissful slumber that awaits you sleeping on 12 inches of mattress, big, bouncy beds which come from Kelletts in Oldcastle.

That is the sort of care and consideration which makes Mrs Colgan's house special. She wants you to be comfortable, she wants you to enjoy a glass of sherry in your room, she wants you to enjoy this lovely old house with its charming furnishings, she wants you to enjoy the feast that is breakfast, and she wants you to go away happy, because then she knows that the next time you have to be in County Meath, like everyone else you will beat a track straight to her door. Aside from the bumper beds, breakfast is the other bumper treat here. Mrs Colgan makes griddle cakes on the slow plate of her Aga – 'They are just crying out for butter!' – she marinates chopped bananas in orange juice and orange zest and cooks them in a sugar syrup; she poaches pears and flavours them with cardamom and ginger; she combines nectarines and peaches; she makes her own granola and serves it with stewed fruits. And that is all before you have some cooked breakfast. It is one of the great feasts to be found, and it's no surprise when she tells you that 'We no longer cook dinner simply because we put so much effort into the breakfast!' Guests tend to eat in Catty Neds in Dunshaughlin, before hurrying back to the Workhouse and that blissful slumber in the deepest mattresses in Ireland.

- **OPEN:** 15 Jan-15 Dec
- **ROOMS:** Four rooms, one suite, all en suite
- **AVERAGE PRICE:** B&B £35-£50 per person sharing, £10-£15 single supplement

- **NOTES:**
Dinner for minimum of six people
Wheelchair Access to ground floor rooms
Children – welcome, but no reduction in price
- On the main N3, Dublin Cavan road, one mile on the Dublin side of Dunshaughlin.

HILTON PARK ©
Johnny & Lucy Madden
Clones, Co Monaghan
Tel: (047) 56007 Fax: 56033
jm@hiltonpark.ie www.hiltonpark.ie

It would be hard to reach a consensus with the diverse and discriminating bunch of folk who use Bridgestone Guides to find great places to stay.. Their tastes – other than for excellent individuality – are difficult to discern. But, if there is one consensus which has slowly been emerging over the last several years, it is that Hilton Park is perhaps the most superb country house of them all. The competition for this title is fierce, for the country houses which feature in this guide have stratospheric standards and are run by talented and committed people. And yet, chatting to readers and receiving letters and e-mails, there is a tendency, amongst people who have enjoyed Lucy and Johnny Madden's exceptional hospitality, their wonderful cooking and the splendours of their extraordinary house, to suggest that Hilton is the one. Perhaps that is the case. What is unarguable, however, is that Hilton is one of the glories of Irish hospitality. It's a lumbering, slumbering pile of a place which the Madden family have inhabited since 1734, though it would be hard to believe that previous generations could have brought as much verve and chutzpah to the house as Johnny and Lucy. Both the house and the 500-acre estate are superbly maintained, and the coup de grâce to all this comfort is some of the most imaginative and excellent country house cooking you can possibly enjoy. Whether or not you agree with the emerging consensus is up to you, but give yourself plenty of time to make your mind up.

● **OPEN:** Apr-Sep
● **ROOMS:** Six rooms, all en suite
● **AVERAGE PRICE:** B&B £64-£75 per person sharing, £10 single supplement. 10% discount if stay Fri & Sat.

● **NOTES:**
Dinner 8pm precisely, £27.50. Separate tables, but communal by mutual arrangement. Book by 10am.
No Wheelchair Access Children – over 8 years welcome.
● From Clones, take the Scotshouse road and the gates to Hilton are on the right after 5km.

10 GREAT HOUSES FOR WEEKENDS

①

ANNAGH LODGE
CO TIPPERARY

②

BOLTOWN HOUSE
CO MEATH

③

THE BROOK LODGE INN
CO WICKLOW

④

GHAN HOUSE
CO LOUTH

⑤

HILTON PARK
CO MONAGHAN

⑥

KILGRANEY HOUSE
CO CARLOW

⑦

LORD BAGENAL INN
CO CARLOW

⑧

THE MOAT INN
NORTHERN IRELAND

⑨

SALVILLE HOUSE
CO WEXFORD

⑩

TEMPLE COUNTRY HOUSE
CO WESTMEATH

COOPERSHILL HOUSE
Brian & Lindy O'Hara
Riverstown, Co Sligo
Tel: (071) 65108 Fax: 65466
ohara@coopershill.com www.coopershill.com

They are great characters, Brian and Lindy O'Hara, and their unpretentious and humorous natures captivate, charm and calm everyone who comes to stay at Coopershill.
It is a particularly fine house, demurely regal, set amidst a 500-acre farm which encloses the house and everyone in it. Coopershill is not far from the main Dublin–Sligo road but, when you turn up here, you enter another universe, an idyll which only the painful cawking of peacocks disrupts.
The house has been home to seven generations of the O'Haras since it was built in 1774, and one can only surmise, given its meticulous, understated, pristine condition, that the O'Haras are and always have been magnificent housekeepers, for Coopershill looks as if it was built yesterday. Spit and polish is clearly the order of the day, and such excellent housekeeping is always reassuring
Brian's bashful sense of humour and Lindy's good cooking complete the picture of a special house. She does classic dishes to perfection – the same eye that keeps the house so pristine is clearly at work in the kitchen – and there are lovely things like Piedmontese roasted peppers, smoked sea trout with quail's eggs and a lemon butter sauce, casserole of venison in red wine, tenderloin of pork with apricots, bumper desserts such as baked stuffed nectarines with mango ice cream, or fresh strawberries with balsamic vinegar, a rich pecan pie. Lovely country cooking in a lovely country house.

- **OPEN:** 1 Apr-31 Oct
- **ROOMS:** Eight rooms, all en suite or private bath
- **AVERAGE PRICE:** B&B £60 per person sharing, £10 single supplement

- **NOTES:**
Dinner 8.30pm, £29-£32
No Wheelchair Access. Children – welcome
Reservations recommended. Vegetarian meals available
- Coopershill is clearly signposted from the Drumfin crossroads on the N4, 11 miles southwest of Sligo.

CROMLEACH LODGE COUNTRY HOUSE
Christy & Moira Tighe
Castlebaldwin, via Boyle, Co Sligo
Tel: (071) 65155 Fax: 65455
info@cromleach.com www.cromleach.com

Cromleach Lodge sits ensconced into a hill overlooking Lough Arrow, in south County Sligo, and as you drive up the hill towards the house, it looks like a building which has, gradually, grown extra layers, sprouted new sections and extensions as the years have gone by.

Inside, whilst the style of the ground floor allows domestic trifles in sitting rooms to clash with professional dining rooms and public spaces, the bedrooms upstairs come as a complete surprise. Huge, super-comfortable and finished to a top-flight specification, they once again challenge your expectations.

In this part of Sligo, you half expected a cosy, daffy country house. In Cromleach, the bedrooms are the equivalent of any top class hotel anywhere in the country. The size and the space, the mattress acreage, the mini-bar, the dauntless views across the slow hills, the sheer gold-tapped splendour of the rooms is a fine surprise, a shock, and a very nice one indeed.

The best surprises come in the restaurant, however, where Mrs Tighe's cooking has never been better. Her confidence has grown over the years, and the complexity of the cooking is now handled with aplomb. Indeed, it's not unusual for people to describe the Cromleach degustation menu as amongst the best food they have enjoyed in Ireland. The ingredients are meticulously sourced, and Mrs Tighe's unclichéd and original style of cooking brings them to their glorious best. The decor of the house doesn't provoke a similar unanimity, however.

- **OPEN:** Feb 1-Nov 1
- **ROOMS:** Ten rooms, all en suite
- **AVERAGE PRICE:** B&B £75-£109, £30 single supplement

- **NOTES:**
Dinner £40. No Wheelchair Access
Children – high chair, cot, babysitting,
private family dining room. Special diets catered for
- Signposted from Castlebaldwin on the N4.

TEMPLE HOUSE ©

Sandy & Deb Perceval
Temple House, Ballymote, Co Sligo
Tel: (071) 83328 Fax: 83808
guest@tempoweb.com
www.templehouse.ie

We all have an idea in our minds as to what the perfect country house break would be like.

There would be a quirky old house full of quirky old things, but it would be comfortable as well as grand, welcoming as well as ancient.

There would be great walking to be had, and maybe fishing and some shooting for them that wants it. And you would look forward to coming back after the day's exertions and peeling off the Barbours and the wellies and plonking yourself down in front of a big fire and having some tea and cake.

And then in the evening there would be a delicious dinner, one where the food was either from the garden, or the farm, or the lake, and where the food spoke of the place itself: a poached salmon; sweet young lamb; peppery beef; floury potatoes and carottes Vichy and jade-green spinach. And the other guests would all be interesting people who you warm to straight away, so much so that when you are leaving cards and e-mail addresses are swopped and you promise to stay in touch.

Reader, it's Temple House you are dreaming of. The dream is a reality. It exists. You can go there.

Sandy and Deb Perceval's glorious old house is like no other. The foods of the garden and the lake and the fields are served for dinner, after that busy day spent fishing or shooting or walking. The other guests are always – but always – fascinating. It's the dream come true, is Temple.

- **OPEN:** 1 Apr-30 Nov
- **ROOMS:** Five rooms, all with private bathrooms
- **AVERAGE PRICE:** B&B £45 per person. Family rates

- **NOTES:**
Residents only Dinner 7.30pm, £20, communal table, book by noon. Vegetarian menu with notice
No Wheelchair Access. Children – welcome, high tea
Important Note: Sandy is very allergic to scented products. Please ask for details when booking.
- Signposted from the N17 Sligo to Galway road.

ANNAGH LODGE
COUNTRY HOUSE

Rachel & Andrew Sterling
Coolbawn, Nenagh, Co Tipperary
Tel & Fax 067 24225
annaghlg@hotmail.com annaghlodge.com

You feel as if you have landed smack in the middle of one of the sets for that great movie, 'Babe', when you find yourself in Annagh Lodge. There is the baby pig, happily snuggled up with the animal he thinks is his mother – the family pet dog. There are the little Kerry Bog ponies, 'like Thellwell's, but without the attitude,' waiting to be ridden and petted. There is the chicken, who thinks she's a family pet, rather than a chicken, and who has to be dissuaded from coming into the house and won't have anything to do with the rest of the flock.

Annagh Lodge is a storybook setting, just made for children, who adore the place. The house itself is simple and uncluttered, with a design aesthetic based simply on being comfortable. Then at the end of the day, everything becomes very civilised. Your kids are off watching television with their kids. The house is calm, and dinner is coming. Rachel is a gifted cook, with a professional flair that tells of her time at Leiths: Broccoli and Stilton Soup, wild duck breast with kumquat casserole, a fantastic chicken and pork terrine, sourced from the Avoca Cookbook, with the house speciality: Cramble Cheese (which is made from the pulp of cranberry and apple jelly). Homemade sausages from their own pigs (oh please, not the little fella who loves the dog!) which she serves with apple sauce, and champ, rhubarb and elderflower crumble made with fruit from the garden. This is hugely sophisticated cooking, and wonderfully pleasing in this natural homely environment. It's a place designed specifically to attract children, but truthfully anyone would find it a happy place to kick-off their shoes.

- **OPEN:** All year
- **ROOMS:** Four rooms, all en suite, two family rooms
- **AVERAGE PRICE:** B&B £24 per person, £30 single

- **NOTES:**
Dinner £22.50, booking essential
No Wheelchair Access. Recommended for children.
- Take the Lough Derg drive north out of Nenagh.

ASHLEY PARK HOUSE

Margaret Mounsey
Nenagh, Co Tipperary
Tel: (067) 38223 Fax: 38013
davidmackenzie@compuserve.com

Something about Ashley Park makes folk want to get on the 'phone the minute they get there.

Just recently, some friends rang on the mobile: 'Just arrived at Ashley Park. It's wonderful. We love it. Great recommendation. Thanks.' And off they went to enjoy themselves some more.

And we first heard about Margaret Mounsey's grand old house from a complete stranger, who never gave their name, and who rang one day and simply said: 'I've just come back from a holiday in Ireland and I found this wonderful place which isn't in your book and I really think it should be. It's near Nenagh, it's called Ashley Park House and I think it's splendid. You should try it. Do you want the telephone number?'

Please.

'You really will like it, I'm sure. I did enjoy using your book. Goodbye.' And the mystery voice rang off.

Ashley Park House looks out over a calm lake, a beautiful location for a handsome house which dates from the 1770's. Ashley Park has a grandeur that is delightful: they simply don't build them on this scale anymore and the bedrooms are the size of suites. It's a lovely house.

But the secret of Ashley Park – the thing that would captivate you – is not the grandeur of the house, but the unpretentious personality of Margaret Mounsey. She has been taking guests for a handful of years now, whilst still managing to rear a family, and there is a wiseness and internationalism about her style, reflecting the confidence of someone who has lived in different parts of the world. A quite lovely house, and don't forget the mobile phone.

● **OPEN:** All year
● **ROOMS:** Six rooms, three en suite
● **AVERAGE PRICE:** B&B £25-£30 per person, £28 single

● **NOTES:**
Dinner by special arrangement
No Wheelchair Access. Children – welcome
● Three miles outside Nenagh, Borrisokane road.

INCH HOUSE
John & Nora Egan
Thurles, Co Tipperary
Tel: (0504) 51261/51348 Fax: 51754
inchhse@iol.ie /www.tipp.ie/inch-house.htm

'They serve good winter food all year round,' is what the locals say about the Egan family's fine Inch House, and in recent times the enjoyable country cooking you find in Inch has helped to create what is very much the destination restaurant of the area. 'It's the place where you find the women in their best blouses,' they say, and indeed a visit to Inch is a treat, a grand night out for everyone.

Michael Doyle has charge of the kitchen, and whilst his food enjoys some modern flourishes – a warm salad of oatmeal-encrusted goat's cheese with yogurt; baked salmon topped with blue poppy seeds served with a beurre blanc – its firmest focus is found when playing to the strengths of the fine local produce – tenderloin of lamb with a Provençal sauce; sirloin steak with red wine and shallot sauce.

The house is located a few miles from the lively town of Thurles, and is a monolithic slab of a building, with a plain exterior that is forbidding. But, then, you walk up the few steps and in through the front door, and suddenly you are embraced by the warm red and blue light streaming through the arching stained glass. You turn right, and walk into a drawing room straight out of that mystical child's imagination which spells William Morris. Across the hallway, the breakfast room, which is transformed in the evening into the dining room, is tall and aristocratic, washed with the soft morning light of Tipperary, and the perfect location for enjoying breakfast, the perfect place for a convivial dinner. Rooms are comfortable, and value for money is excellent.

● **OPEN:** All year, except Christmas
● **ROOMS:** Five rooms, all en suite
● **AVERAGE PRICE:** B&B £35 per person sharing, £5 single supplement

● **NOTES:**
Dinner 7pm-9.30pm Tue-Sat, £27
No Wheelchair Access. Children – welcome, cot, high chair, babysitting on request
● Four miles from Thurles on the Nenagh Road.

LEGENDS TOWNHOUSE & RESTAURANT

Michael & Rosemary O'Neill
The Kiln, Cashel, Co Tipperary
Tel: (062) 61292 www.legendsguesthouse.com
info@legendsguesthouse.com

Legends Townhouse and its restaurant, The Kiln, are run by Michael and Rosemary O'Neill, and you will have to walk a very lengthy country mile indeed to find a couple who are more assured in their work than this ultra-professional pair.

Mrs O'Neill works front of house with considerable grace, setting the tone of the cosy and comfortable dining room at a calm but fizzy pitch. Mr O'Neill cooks, and he is a serious cook indeed, with a mature and disciplined style of food that is spot on: simple starters such as black pudding with caramelised apples and potato cakes; benchmark twice-baked cheese soufflé; smoked cod fritters with aioli; rack of lamb with button onions and rosemary sauce; grilled fillet of beef with scallion potatoes (whatever happened to good old champ?!); classic desserts such as warm chocolate pudding. Fine cooking which the gracious service makes even more fun to enjoy.

But the coup de grâce is that this lovely food is enjoyed in a room that looks directly out on the glorious Rock of Cashel: The Kiln is directly underneath Ireland's most amazing historical landmark, which towers ominously and gloriously over the house.

And, having enjoyed dinner, you simply head upstairs to your room, prop yourself up in bed, and lie looking straight out at this extraordinary monolith. The rooms are simple – pine furniture, decent bathrooms – and are being personalised and steadily upgraded as time goes by.

● **OPEN:** All year (except two weeks in Nov & Feb)
● **ROOMS:** Seven rooms, all en suite
● **AVERAGE PRICE:** B&B £25-£35 per person sharing, £5 single supplement

● **NOTES:**
The Kiln Restaurant, Mon-Sun £23-£26 (early evening menus, Sun lunch, £15). No Wheelchair Access. Children – family rooms, but no children under 10 years in restaurant. Vegetarian and special diets catered for.
● From N7 take R660 to Holy Cross, fourth house on left.

ANNESTOWN HOUSE
John & Pippa Galloway
Annestown, Co Waterford
Tel: (051) 396160 Fax: 396474
relax@annestown.com www.annestown.com

Annestown enjoys a truly lovely location, beside the sea and adjacent to a sandy beach on this overlooked part of the Waterford coastline. This is a bracing, invigorating stretch of the shoreline, someplace that makes you want to set out on an invigorating trek to brave the elements. John and Pippa Galloway have a professional background in the people business, and indeed they formerly ran Annestown as a restaurant. Between them they have lots of patiently acquired experience, and it gives their work an extra polish, a confidence and understatement.

Above all, it is the air of nostalgia which clings to the house itself that makes it special. The sitting room with its flame-lapping fire is the sort of place that demands you sit right down and take tea, and chat and discuss the day. The snooker room, ringed with shelf after shelf of handsome volumes – 'two yards of Voltaire, all in French!,' laughs John Galloway – makes you want to pick up a glass of brandy and brandish a cue, and the dining room is the sort of place where you want to congregate with your friends over a weekend dinner, enjoying Pippa's good cooking, transforming the place into a country house weekend. The Galloways enjoy their guests and, vitally, enjoy their guests enjoying the house. As a place for walking, exploring, whacking some croquet out on the lawn, or just chilling out and doing not much of anything save having a fine time, Annestown fits the bill.

- **OPEN:** 1 March-31 Oct
(house parties accepted off season)
- **ROOMS:** Five rooms, all en suite
- **AVERAGE PRICE:** B&B £40 per person sharing, £15 single supplement

- **NOTES:**
Dinner 7.45pm Mon-Sat, £23.
No Wheelchair Access
Children – welcome, high chairs, cots, babysitting
Enclosed car parking. No smoking in bedrooms
- Take Tramore road from Waterford, and Annestown is 9km west of Tramore. The house is signposted.

BUGGY'S GLENCAIRN INN

Ken & Cathleen Buggy
Glencairn, Co Waterford
Tel: (058) 56232 Fax: 56232
buggysglencairninn@eircom.net
www.lismore.com or www.buggys.net

Poor old Ken Buggy. He's become such a popular figure that he's almost a part of the Establishment. He is asked to give speeches now, and when he does folk sit there and listen and pay attention and applaud. Applause! Sure, we knew him when all he could expect was heckles and hisses!

You will find the great and the good staying and eating in Buggy's at any given time, drawn here by the whackyness and wildness and inimitability of the Glencairn Inn. The fact that Mr Buggy is a thoroughly out-of-the-box character no longer seems to strike people as strange. They have gotten so used to accepting the environment of Buggy's, they have become so in love with hearing about the world through Ken Buggy's eyes, that they love him regardless. Someone should make a movie about him (someone almost certainly will) and it should be similar to Spike Jonze's excellent feature, 'Being John Malkovich'. Malkovich is strange, but everyone accepts his strangeness, and wants it. It's the same with Ken Buggy. He thinks differently from the rest of us – hell, he does everything different from the rest of us. And we crave that uniqueness, that strangeness. We want some of it, we want to stroll through that surreal subconscious.

We want it because Mr Buggy is so good, and because he has the courage to be original. Buggy's Glencairn Inn is like no other place you have ever stayed in, eaten in or drank in. It's extraordinary.

- **OPEN:** All year, except Christmas
- **ROOMS:** Five rooms, all en suite
- **AVERAGE PRICE:** B&B £32-£36 per person sharing, £10 single supplement

- **NOTES:**
Dinner from 7.30pm, booking advisable, £21
Off street car parking. No Wheelchair Access
Children – welcome, but no facilities
- In Lismore turn right at monument, drive to Horneybrooks garage, look for sign to Glencairn.

HANORA'S COTTAGE Ⓒ
Seamus & Mary Wall
Nire Valley, Clonmel, Co Waterford
Tel: (052) 36134 Fax: 36540

When you walk in to Nora and Seamus Wall's handsome Hanora's Cottage, take a minute to look at the framed photograph of the small cottage which is hanging on the wall close to the reception desk. You may find it difficult to believe, as you look around you at this comforting and elegant restaurant with rooms, that the photograph is of the original Hanora's Cottage, the modest beginning out of which this splendid family business has steadily and organically grown to its impressive present state.

But the Wall family's patient and inexorable search for improvement, the endless demand for excellence which has marked their three decades of work, is apparent in every detail of Hanora's Cottage. The key feature of their legendary breakfasts, a kaleidoscope of the finest local foods from farmhouse cheeses and smoked salmon through to Nora Wall's fabulous porridge, is not merely that it is amongst the greatest breakfasts served anywhere in the country, but that this lavish and epic feast is offered whether two people or twenty people are staying in the house.

Mary and Seamus' son Eoin, and his wife Judith, now run the restaurant, and the culinary energy of this young couple is expressed in marvellously rootsy, flavourful cooking: celery and Cashel Blue cheese soup; oven-baked brill with a tomato and cheese crust; marinated breast of Englishtown chicken with lemon, garlic and basil; apple and almond crumble with crème anglaise; walnut tart with vanilla ice cream, an elegant culinary fugue to the fabulous prelude of pleasure that is breakfast. Superb rooms, and the Nire valley is a walker's paradise.

● **OPEN:** All year, except Christmas
● **ROOMS:** Eleven rooms, four with jacuzzi bath, two with bathrooms
● **AVERAGE PRICE:** B&B £45-£65 per person sharing, £20 single supplement

● **NOTES:**
Dinner 6.30pm–9pm, £30
Wheelchair Access. No children. Off street car parking
● From Clonmel or Dungarvan, follow signs to
Ballymaclery village, the house is signposted from there.

RICHMOND HOUSE ©
The Deevy family
Cappoquin, Co Waterford
Tel: (058) 54278 Fax: 54988
richmondhouse.net info@richmondhouse.net

Do you know what is one of the nicest things about Richmond House?

Bringing someone here who has never seen it before, is the answer. Let them walk first into the old-style entrance hall, with its fireplace, its little reception desk, the staircase peeling away to the rere, and you can see them being captivated by the realness, the genuineness, the lack of pretension of this fine country house on the outskirts of Cappoquin.

And they go to their room and love the simple comfort, and meet Claire Deevy and are captivated by her quiet charm. And then at dinnertime they are simply gob-smacked by Paul Deevy's thunderous country cooking: real food from a really good cook: smoked duck breast with roast beetroot; potato and thyme soup; veal fillet with a port and tarragon gravy; fillet of brill with a herb butter sauce; local raspberries with homemade ice cream. And the service by local ladies and by Claire Deevy is just so right, the peaceful atmosphere of the dining room relaxing and informal. There are fishermen, and local families, and courting couples, all having a thoroughly lovely time, thank you very much.

It's a pleasure to be able to introduce someone to the pleasures of Richmond. But, of course, it is vitally important that you yourself are there to register their delight and to report on it. No point in letting them get on with having a high old time without you, after all. That wouldn't do at all. Perish the thought.

- **OPEN:** 20 Jan-23 Dec
- **ROOMS:** Nine rooms, all en suite
- **AVERAGE PRICE:** B&B £45-£80 per person sharing, £10 single supplement

- **NOTES:**
Dinner 7pm-9pm, £32 (or a la carte)
No Wheelchair Access
Children – welcome, high chairs and cots
Enclosed car parking. Recommended for Vegetarians
- Just outside Cappoquin, the house is well signposted.

GORTNADIHA HOUSE
Eileen & Tom Harty
Ring, Dungarvan, Co Waterford
Tel: (058) 46142
ringcheese@eircom.net

Eileen Harty will be known to many people as one of the Harty family who for many years made the much-loved Ring Farmhouse Cheese, on the family farm at Gortnadiha House.

The cheese is currently not in production, unfortunately, but anyone who misses the relish for her task which Mrs Harty brought to being a cheesemaker will be consoled by the fact that, should you choose to stay in the comfortable, swaddling confines of Gortnadiha, in the Irish-speaking Gaeltacht area of Ring, then that same irrepressible spirit is as alive and well in Mrs Harty's new found vocation as hostess.

'I adore it,' she says, simple as that. 'I feel I've found my niche. What I love is to have four or six people I can talk to and have a nice drink with. Some mornings they aren't out of the house before 11 o'clock!'

Aside from the craic, what will be delaying your planned early start will be the handsome Harty breakfast. Fresh orange juice. Pancakes and maple syrup. Pink grapefruit with melon balls. Toasted homemade muesli. Smoked herrings from West Cork's inimitable fish smoker, Sally Barnes. Free range eggs scrambled with smoked salmon. Fried bread with black pudding, bacon and stewed apple. A board of Irish farmhouse cheeses.

The house itself is tall and welcoming, with a cavernous fire roaring in the sitting room, and the rooms are big and cosy, expertly decorated. Expect to leave late, in the morning. And expect to return as early and as often as you possibly can.

● **OPEN:** Mid Mar-mid Nov
● **ROOMS:** Three rooms, all en suite
● **AVERAGE PRICE:** B&B £25 per person sharing, £10 single supplement

● **NOTES:**
No Dinner
No Wheelchair Access
Children – welcome
● 7km from Dungarvan, on the Ring peninsula.

TEMPLE COUNTRY HOUSE& HEALTH SPA ©

Declan & Bernadette Fagan
Horseleap, Moate, Co Westmeath
Tel: (0506) 35118 Fax: 35008
www.templespa.ie info@templespa.ie

There are two schools of thought about the business of creating a spa. The first suggests that the way to do it is to throw a great wad of money into a brand new building beside the sea and to pack it with every manner of treatment. Once this is done, the punters will surely roll up like lemmings heading for those beachy cliffs.

But there is another way to do it, if you look at the example of Bernadette and Declan Fagan's celebrated Temple.

For starters, Temple is in the middle of the country, a stone's throw back from the main Dublin-Galway road. For another, it's set in a fine old house, from which it has grown and extended in recent years. And rather than building a spa from the ground up, the Fagans have patiently built Temple piece by piece. And the range of spa treatments has developed over the years, and has recently necessitated the building of new treatment rooms.

And the house itself has been improved, steadily and organically, so that its elegance and comfort and period details are respected. The eight rooms are all inspiringly comfortable, their style judged expertly. And whilst this steady, organic progress has been taking place, Mrs Fagan has retained her sense of enquiry and her nuanced creativity when it comes to cooking. The food in Temple is true spa food, inasmuch as it is: food which makes you feel better. So, what happens if you build a spa the Fagan way? Why, you wind up with the finest and best-loved spa in Ireland, that's what.

- ● **OPEN:** Mid Jan-mid Dec
- ● **ROOMS:** Eight rooms, all en suite
- ● **AVERAGE PRICE:** Inclusive rates, full board and a limited number of treatments, £215-£325, single supplement £10-£20 per night

- ● **NOTES:**
Dinner 8pm, £20, communal table book by 10am (dinner included in weekend rate). Spa facilities by appointment. No Wheelchair Access.
Children – welcome in school holidays only
- ● Half a mile off the N6, clearly signposted.

KELLY'S RESORT HOTEL
Bill Kelly
Rosslare, Co Wexford
Tel: (053) 32114 Fax: 32222
kellyhot@iol.ie www.kellys.ie

'But Kelly's isn't fashionable with the dot.com set, is it?' asks a friend.

It's an interesting remark, and it proves a couple of interesting points about Kelly's.

Firstly, it shows that some folk have a perception that Bill Kelly's hotel is some sort of place down in the south-east where retired genteel folk head to, to get some sun and some golf. Some just don't realise that Kelly's is as cutting-edge as it gets.

The hotel has one of the most magnificent collections of modern Irish paintings you will find anywhere. Its bedrooms – thanks to an endless round of refurbishment which takes place every winter when the hotel closes for a few weeks – are as swish and comfortable as you could hope for. The design features of the bar are as cool as any Dublin club, and the swimming pool and the sports facilities are state-of-the-art.

The cooking in the hotel is excellent, thanks to the fact that head chef Jim Ahearne has inexhaustible energy, and in La Marine bistro, Eugene Callaghan continues to prove to everyone that he is one of the great chefs of his generation. And a word about the service: you simply will not find better service anywhere else in the country.

But the remark also proves that, yes, Kelly's is not a fashionable place. It isn't fashionable simply because it transcends fashion. Kelly's is all about style, not fashion. It is about the great civilising culture of food and wine and hospitality, and these things are beyond fashion. The dot.com set will discover that one of these days.

● **OPEN:** Late Feb-early Dec
● **ROOMS:** Ninety nine rooms, all en suite
● **AVERAGE PRICE:** Accommodation is quoted on a two-day, five-day or seven-day basis, full board. See their website or telephone for individual rates.

● **NOTES:**
Dinner 7.30pm-9pm
Full Wheelchair Access. Children – welcome
● Clearly signposted in Rosslare.

10 GREAT NEW DISCOVERIES

①
ANNAGH LODGE
CO TIPPERARY

②
DOLPHIN BEACH
CO GALWAY

③
FITZWILLIAM PARK HOTEL
CO DUBLIN

④
GLENALLY HOUSE
CO CORK

⑤
THE GREEN GATE
CO DONEGAL

⑥
IVYLEIGH HOUSE
CO LAOIS

⑦
THE MILL HOUSE RESTAURANT
CO DONEGAL

⑧
THE MOAT INN
NORTHERN IRELAND

⑨
SIMMONSTOWN HOUSE
CO DUBLIN

⑩
STRANGFORD COTTAGE
NORTHERN IRELAND

McMENAMIN'S TOWNHOUSE
Seamus & Kay McMenamin
3 Auburn Terrace, Redmond Road, Wexford
Tel: (053) 46442
mcmem@indigo.ie
www.wexford-bedandbreakfast.com

They are generous people, Seamus and Kay McMenamin, and their generosity explains why McMenamin's is such a success.

There is generosity in the welcome, the chat, the exchange of news and views, the 'Well, how are you and what sort of a day have you had?' There is generosity in the advice, the help in booking somewhere in Wexford town for dinner (the house is only a few minutes' walk from the city centre), in arranging ferries and other travel details, in helping with other places to stay.

And there is generosity in the breakfast, which is one of the best you will find. Everyone, but everyone, loves the porridge with the halo of rum, but some will rate the devilled kidneys even better than that, whilst others are delighted to be offered fresh fish for breakfast: last time we were here it was fine fillets of haddock, cooked to perfection, and served simply with lemon, which was all the fish needed.

But then those are only some parts of the breakfast feast. There is also good poached fruit, served with organic yogurt. There are five or six types of bread, including s super Guinness bread (rum in the porridge? Guinness in the bread? Blimey!) and there is lots of chat, and newspapers to peruse, and the comfort of the room to be enjoyed.

The rooms are very comfortable, and some have extremely interesting old beds. For many people, McMenamin's is the only place they would consider staying when in Wexford, and it is easy to see why they come back time and again.

- **OPEN:** All year, except Christmas
- **ROOMS:** Five rooms, all en suite
- **AVERAGE PRICE:** B&B £30 per person, £35 single

- **NOTES:**
No Dinner. No Wheelchair Access. Locked parking
Children – welcome, high chair, cot, babysitting
- In the centre of Wexford, directly opposite
bus/railway stations, beside Dunnes Stores.

SALVILLE HOUSE

Jane & Gordon Parker
Enniscorthy, Co Wexford
Tel: (054) 35252 Fax: 35252
salvillehouse@eircom.net www.salvillehouse.com

Things find their right place in Salville, this adorable house up on the hill just outside Enniscorthy. Jane and Gordon Parker know what belongs where, and their very elemental attitude to furnishing, their understanding of arrangement and tactility, is what creates the easeful sense of comfort in this spiffing house.

The decor is spiffing, and so is Gordon Parker's cooking. Salville offers some of the nicest and truest and most enjoyable country house cooking you can find in Ireland: summer vegetable soup with herbs (those herbs collated from the garden just before dinner); fillet of cod with spinach and pink fir apple potatoes; tarragon chicken with straw potatoes; vanilla pavlova with red fruit coulis.

Mr Parker really understands his food, and his use of herbs, in particular, bespeaks a mature, confident and expressive cook. And to eat dinner in the lovely dining room, with its enormous windows, is a true treat

The Parkers have most recently developed a cottage adjacent to the main house, again simply and appropriately decorated, with ornamentation kept to a minimum. There are two bedrooms here, a sitting room, kitchen and bathroom, all with the same simple grace as the main house. This sense of grace is the secret of Salville, and the Parkers complement the poise of their lovely house. Like all the great hosts, the Parkers create their own aesthetic with everything they touch. Nothing is ever taken for granted. Salville is individualistic, inspiring, an oasis.

● **OPEN:** All year
● **ROOMS:** Three rooms, all with private bath.
● **AVERAGE PRICE:** B&B £27.50 per person sharing. £5 single supplement

● **NOTES:**
Dinner, with 24hrs notice, £22.50 communal table. BYO. Private apartment priced seasonally. Wheelchair Access to private apartment only. Children – all facilities
● Just off the N11 to Wexford – take the first left after the hospital, go up the hill to a T-junction then turn left and proceed for half km.

VALE VIEW
Mary Keogh
St John's, Enniscorthy, Co Wexford
Tel: (054) 35262

'I've had people staying here, and when they were leaving they said to me: "The Lord sent us here"', says Mary Keogh. Speaking to the dynamic Mrs Keogh, one can understand the reaction: she is a true Good Samaritan, who loves looking after people in her simple little bungalow, set in the midst of beautiful St John's. 'I've never had one stay here who was grumpy,' says Mary, and who could be downcast in the presence of this human whirlwind. In fact, the folk who come here – golfers, musicians, holidaymakers, weekenders – are so happy that they all come back. 'There was a Guard staying who used to go to the fleadh in Enniscorthy and play three instruments, and he would come back here and play for everyone. And people would ask, 'Did you go to the fleadh, Mary?' and I would say: 'No, the fleadh came to me.'

Mrs Keogh's success is based on a simple principle: basically, she mothers everyone, young and old. 'I've had them from a 2-year-old child to an 89-year-old woman,' and everyone is offered her fine fruit loaf with some tea, everyone is offered sandwiches on her little verandah, everyone writes and thanks her when they return home, and most likely send a gift as well. 'Look at these, arrived today,' and she shows a whole box of tulip bulbs, posted by a Dutch visitor. 'All I did was mention I liked tulips!'

The house is as simple and unpretentious as you might imagine, with just three rooms. But Mrs Keogh, who took to running the business when her husband passed away, makes any sort of consideration of 'luxury' an irrelevance. The luxury here is in the goodness of heart, and the torrent of generous, unselfconscious hospitality.

● **OPEN:** All year, except Christmas
● **ROOMS:** Three rooms, two en suite
● **AVERAGE PRICE:** B&B £20-£25 per person sharing, £10 single supplement

● **NOTES:**
Dinner £15-£20, BYO
Wheelchair Access. Children – welcome
● Signposted from both the N30 and N11.

THE BROOK LODGE INN

Evan, Eoin & Bernard Doyle
Macreddin Village, Co Wicklow
Tel: (0402) 36444 Fax: (0402) 36580
brooklodge@macreddin.ie www.brooklodge.com

There are many remarkable things about The Brook Lodge Inn. There is its amazing cooking. Its subtle stylishness. Its excellent staff. Its marvellous location. Its romantic little church. Its little microbrewery in Actons Pub. The initiative that is its regular weekend markets. Its elegant public rooms. Its intimate bedrooms.

But the most remarkable thing about The Brook Lodge Inn is this: how on earth did Evan Doyle and Freda Wolfe even begin to imagine this unique concept? How did they have the nerve to even dream about a super country hotel and restaurant which could be created out of a green field site in Wicklow, seemingly in the space of a few months, and which could then so swiftly establish itself as one of the best places to eat and stay in Ireland? What sort of wild willpower do you need in order to come up with this extraordinary creation.

One can only explain it in terms used in modern management analysis: as a concept, The Brook Lodge is a piece of thinking that is Out Of The Box. It is so outrageous to believe that you can build an hotel with a little village of shops and a pub, and to do it from scratch, that the only thing to do with such a wild idea is... to get on and do it. That is what Doyle and Wolfe have done. Where once there was a set of fields in deepest Wicklow, there is now one of the most admirable places to offer hospitality anywhere in the country. It's outrageous. Remarkable. Best of all, it is very, very good indeed.

- **OPEN:** All year
- **ROOMS:** Forty rooms, all en suite
- **AVERAGE PRICE:** B&B £65-£80 per person sharing, £20 single supplement

- **NOTES:**
The Strawberry Tree restaurant, microbrewery & bars
Enclosed car park. Wheelchair Access. Equestrian centre.
Children – welcome
Six retail units, incl. shop, bakery, smokehouse.
- Follow signs from Aughrim (3 kms). Total journey, one hour south of Dublin centre.

RATHSALLAGH HOUSE
The O'Flynn family
Dunlavin, Co Wicklow
Tel: (045) 53112 Fax: 53343
info@rathsallagh.com
www.rathsallagh.com

The country house phenomenon in Ireland has been slowing down in recent years, as some of the original owners run out of steam or begin to step back and take it easy and pass the business on to a new generation.

But in Rathsallagh, Joe and Kay O'Flynn's energy seems boundless, and this elegant big house and its 500-odd acres continues to power its way forward.

It now boasts a championship golf course with a country club in the grounds, but it should be said that whilst golfers are attracted to Rathsallagh, it is the charms of the house itself and the cooking which draw people back time and again. Rathsallagh is comfortable, and relaxing, and offers the quintessential country house experience, albeit at fairly steep prices. Best of all, it's not some slick operation: it may be big, but it always feels like a home.

However, those prices don't seem to phase the folk who come here, probably because they only have to walk through the doors to switch off, bliss out and enter an exalted state of economic unconsciousness. And Niall Hill's generous, tasty cooking merely stokes up the feeling of comfort and pampering. He is fortunate to have Rathsallagh's walled garden to provide much of the produce used in the kitchen, which gives a purity to his work that is rounded out by good meat and game cookery.

Breakfast is a positively Gothic experience, an epicurean indulgence with seemingly limitless amounts of food on offer from the sideboard, with its centrepiece of an enormous ham on the bone surrounded by all the other breakfast dishes you crave but simply would never make for yourself.

● **OPEN:** All year, except Christmas
● **ROOMS:** Seventeen rooms, all en suite
● **AVERAGE PRICE:** B&B £55-£105 per person sharing, £30-£50 single supplement

● **NOTES:**
Dinner £35-£40. Enclosed car park. Wheelchair Access. Children – over 12 years welcome
● Signposted in Dunlavin village, 1 hour from Dublin.

TINAKILLY HOUSE HOTEL

Josephine & Raymond Power
Rathnew, Co Wicklow
Tel: (0404) 69274 Fax: 67806
reservations@tinakilly.ie
www.tinakilly.ie

It was all change at Tinakilly last year.

William and Bee Power passed on the reins to their son and daughter-in-law, Raymond and Josephine, and it is the younger Mrs Power who is now host in this fine, noble old country house hotel.

There was change in the kitchen also, with Chris Bailey taking over the role to which John Moloney had brought such distinction for a decade. Mr Bailey's cooking is ambitious – gratin of crab and citrus fruits with citrus sabayon; magret of duck on hazelnut mash with cassis and forest fruits; pineapple and cashew nut spring roll on a white chocolate sauce – but at present it lacks a distinct signature and some discipline.

Other key staff members such as Catherine Fulvio also moved on to new ventures, in Mrs Fulvio's case the running of her own country house, Ballyknocken House, in Ashford, a few miles away.

But manageress Louise Barry and other pivotal team members are still here and still as personable as ever, and they have been working hard with Josephine Power to maintain the focus of Tinakilly.

This is no easy task, for Bill Power was one of the great Irish hoteliers, a man who brought nothing less than artistry to his calling and who bestowed a democratic paternalism on Tinakilly which was always one of its most beguiling features. But whilst changes have been taking place, the house itself remains charming and comfortable, elegantly and understatedly furnished.

● **OPEN:** All year, including Christmas
● **ROOMS:** Fifty five rooms and suites, all en suite
● **AVERAGE PRICE:** B&B £74 per person sharing, single supplement £48

● **NOTES:**
Dinner 7.30pm-9pm, £39. Vegetarian options.
Private car parking. Reservations essential.
No Wheelchair Access. Children – welcome
● From N11, bear left in Rathnew village.

NORTHERN IRELAND

ASH ROWAN

Evelyn & Sam Hazlett
12 Windsor Avenue, Belfast, BT9 6EE
Tel: (028) 9066 1758/9066 1983 Fax: 9066 3227
ashrowan@hotmail.com

Sam and Evelyn. This is what Ash Rowan is all about, and discovering that this is what the Ash Rowan is all about is something you discover pretty much the second you walk through the door.

Sam and Evelyn greet and meet, advise and cook, chat and speculate, gossip and inform. After about 90 seconds you reckon you have known them for half your life. They have that mixture of discretion and intuition which is so fiendishly hard to get right, that instinctive hospitality that you probably have to be born with, for there doesn't seem to be any way in which you can learn it.

Much as Evelyn might suggest that good cooks are born, not made, you have to reckon that in the Ash Rowan they show that good hospitality is in the blood. It's just a way of doing things right – with attention to detail, with respect for their own work – which makes the place special. It's no surprise, then, that the road-weary crew who are the classical musicians of the world should so assiduously colonise the Ash Rowan.

With its politely understated decor, its slightly distressed grouting, its element of mix-match and steady accumulation, its collation of private memorabilia arranged here and there, it's a house where it is easy to lay your head.

Evelyn is a good cook, and a woman with a very true appreciation of good food. Breads, coffee and – above all – her scrambled eggs, enjoy the sure touch of someone who loves food and can't tolerate doing something by rote. It is the final element in a house which has the sort of relaxed character that makes you want to linger for a few days, thanks to Sam and Evelyn.

- ● **OPEN:** All year, except Christmas
- ● **ROOMS:** Six rooms, all en suite
- ● **AVERAGE PRICE:** B&B £33-£42 per person sharing, £10 single supplement

● **NOTES:**
Dinner 7pm, £25, separate tables. Locked car parking No Wheelchair Access. Children – over 12 years welcome
● Go through Bradbury Place on to University road. Windsor Ave is the 3rd Ave on right past the Botanic Inn.

MADDYBENNY FARMHOUSE
Rosemary White
18 Maddybenny Park, Portrush, Co Antrim
Tel: (028) 7082 3394 Fax: 7082 3394
accommodation@maddybenny22.freeserve.co.uk
www.maddybenny.freeserve.co.uk./

The years seem to have little or no impact on Rosemary White. From the simple beginnings of the flower-bedecked farmhouse where guests still stay, there has grown a handsome collection of red and white-painted cottages, which are perfect for family holidays, and a very serious equestrian centre.

She continues to cook one of the most extraordinary breakfasts you can enjoy anywhere in Ireland, a feast of such epic proportions that it almost assumes the status of a religious experience.

You order this feast the night before, for this little bit of notice allows Mrs White to cook everything as freshly as possible. This has always been one of the pivotal things about the success of her cooking – the sheer zing and zip of those good hot bangers and bacon straight from the pan is what counts.

But there is a lot more before we get to the bangers and bacon. There are chilled juices, grapefruit and other seasonal fruits according to the time of year; cereals and muesli, and her amazing porridge served the Maddybenny Way, with runny honey and a halo of Drambuie or Irish Mist liqueur. Then, in addition to the Golfer's fry, which features Mrs White's award-winning fadge – the Ulster term for potato cakes – there are sausage and bacon kebabs, spiced lamb's kidneys; cocktail sausages and potato pancake for the kids, and there are both local trout and kippers on offer. If, for some reason, you aren't tempted by all this, then you can choose a continental breakfast, or American waffles with real maple syrup. Extraordinary, there's no other word for it.

● **OPEN:** All year, except Christmas
● **ROOMS:** Three rooms, all en suite
Six self-catering cottages also available
● **AVERAGE PRICE:** B&B £25-£27.50 per person sharing

● **NOTES:**
No Dinner. Enclosed parking. No Wheelchair Access.
Children – welcome, high chair, cot
● Signed from the A29 Coleraine/Portrush road.

THE MOAT INN ❷

Robert & Rachel Thompson
12 Donegore Hill, Templepatrick
Co Antrim BT41 2HW
Tel: (028) 9443 3659 Fax: (028) 9443 3726
themoatinn@talk21.com

Has any other house seen as many different lives as the lovely Moat Inn? Since it was first built in 1740, it has been a pub, a dance hall, a private house and now, under the careful and tasteful care of Robert and Rachel Thompson, it is a splendiferous little country house.

It's a dreamy tone poem of a place, the entrance room deep red with a roaring old fire, the dining room small and cool with both a piano (both Robert and Rachel are musicians, he even being church organist for St Peters on the Antrim Road in Belfast) and a smashing French dining table dating from the 1880's. The intimacy of the house is the distinguishing feature of the downstairs, especially the little blue drawing room with its Victorian slate fireplace. Upstairs, the bedrooms are diverse, though it would be hard not to plump for the four-poster bedroom as an especial favourite. But the design features this enthusiastic pair have collected and collated are put to effective and memorable use, and their particular affection for Victoriana works perfectly in the low-ceilinged context.

Cooking is another passion along with interiors, which means that Mrs Thompson has already established an impressive reputation for her dinner cooking: maple-marinaded chicken millefeuille with red onion marmalade; parsnip and chorizo soup; salmon filo parcels with dill and lemon butter; caramelised citrus tart with dark berry ice cream; cheeses with biscuits and homemade chutney was a late-winter dinner menu one evening, and gives some idea of the imaginative accomplishment you will enjoy.

- **OPEN:** All year
- **ROOMS:** Three rooms, all en suite
- **AVERAGE PRICE:** B&B £30 per person

- **NOTES:**
Candlelight dinner £18, High Tea £10
Dinner parties for non residents, £25 per person
Picnic hamper on request. Free airport transfer
Wheelchair Access. Children welcome
- Beside the church at Donegore.

BEECH HILL COUNTRY HOUSE
Victoria Brann
23 Ballymoney Road, Craigantlet, Newtownards,
Co Down, Northern Ireland
Tel: (028) 9042 5892 Fax: 9042 5892
www.beech-hill.net beech.hill@btinternet.com

Beech Hill is the sort of house that a style editor for a magazine such as Country Living would not merely drool over, but would likely die for. It is quite lovely, with formal rooms eliding into the informal rooms with great architectural panache, with Victoria Brann's furnishings displayed with taste and restraint, with an atmosphere that persuades you to sit right down and stay put for as long as you can.

To achieve this is no accident. Ms Brann is a stickler for attention to detail. We once overheard her explaining to an assistant exactly how a tea tray must be correctly arranged before it is brought out to a guest, and that is the sort of care and professionalism you can expect when staying here.

Curiously, then, Ms Brann will explain of the business of having guests that, 'I don't think of this as work,' but that is simply because she has that capacity to do a zillion things at any one given time which is the halo of anyone who has ever worked in the food business (she is Cordon Bleu trained). 'I treat everyone like a house party guest, and introduce them all to one another,' she says, and that happy atmosphere is a pivotal part of the charm of Beech Hill, along with the comfort, the design, the architectural style, and the welcome. Do note that there are exceptionally good restaurants, such as Shanks and Fontana, quite proximate to the house, so dinner is easily arranged.

- **OPEN:** All year
- **ROOMS:** Three rooms, all en suite
- **AVERAGE PRICE:** B&B £30 per person sharing, £10 single supplement

- **NOTES:**
No Dinner. Enclosed parking. Wheelchair Access (ground floor rooms), but no special disabled facilities Children – welcome, high chair, cot. Dogs welcome
- 1.5 miles after the Ulster Folk Museum (on A2) turn right up Ballymoney road, signed Craigantlet.

STRANGFORD COTTAGE
Maureen Thornton
Strangford, Co Down BT30 7NF
Tel: (028) 4488 1208 Fax: (028) 4488 1246

'It all started thanks to the Castleward opera season,' says Maureen Thornton. 'They needed someone to put up their rehearsal pianist, and since then it's all been word of mouth over the last 5 years.'

If Strangford Cottage owes its professional existence to a theatrical-operatic initiation, then you couldn't possibly find a more appropriate place. The very style of this house is grandly theatrical, none more so than the imposing sitting room with its deep red walls, massive fireguard (straight out of some early Hitchcock movie) and plush seating. But you move next door to the breakfast room, and now it's time to admire the restraint of this small room, its apposite colouring, its demureness. The bedrooms are no less theatrical, with their fine Colefax & Fowler, the dramatic bath in the centre of the room, the confident plash of the colours, the superbly comfortable garden room which is let during the summer and which boasts an impressive canvas and a delightful wall-hanging made by Maureen herself.

Mrs Thornton's husband works in Dublin in the theatrical world, and she herself has the self-aware posture of an actress. This appreciation of design and staging makes for a special house, one which is no less than 200 years old, and a place which enjoys a superb location high on the hill overlooking the harbour in Strangford. 'Maureen really cares about the food, and it shows,' wrote some friends who described a breakfast dish of cod with herbs as simply 'melting in the mouth' whilst fresh fruits with sorbet was sublime. 'We could go on and on...' they wrote, and doubtless you will.

- ● **OPEN:** All year
- ● **ROOMS:** Three rooms, all en suite
- ● **AVERAGE PRICE:** B&B £40 per person, £10 single supplement

● **NOTES:**
Dinner by arrangement
No Credit Cards. Wheelchair Access
No facilities for children
● 12 miles beyond Downpatrick.

INDEX

NOTES

To find out
all you
need to know

about
Estragon Press
Publishing

& the
Bridgestone
Guides

visit...

bridgestoneguides.com

Megabytes.ie

...is a **FREE** witty, up-to-the-minute e-zine, written by John McKenna and various contributors from the world of food, both Irish and international.

visit:

bridgestoneguides.com and sign up!

Megabytes.ie

Features include:

• **Up-to-date information about the world of Irish food**

• **Regular campaigns to protect our food culture**

• **Monthly recipes**

• **A look at menus from both Ireland and abroad**

• **Features by some of Ireland's leading chefs**

• **Readers' reports**

• **Competitions with great foodie prizes**

• **Special offers**

• **A free noticeboard for the trade buying and selling anything from a front-of-house to a side of organic pork!**

• **And much much more...**

Other titles from Estragon Press...

The companion volume to this book is:

● Irish cooking has never been more exciting or more enjoyable. The Bridgestone 100 Best Restaurants in Ireland 2001 will guide you to the most creative and cutting-edge restaurants throughout the country.

● The book features grand city restaurants, and tiny little one-room restaurants in the wilds of the country. There are restaurants located on islands, and restaurants that reverberate with the energy and mania of the city.

'Thanks to your book we did not have a bad meal in Ireland'

● Written in a vivid and humorous style which has won great critical acclaim, the Guide not only gives details of the finest restaurants, B&Bs, country houses, and hotels, but uniquely

offers a guide to the artisan food producers who have revolutionised the quality of Irish food in the last decade.

ISBN 1 874076 32 4

● The fifth edition of this pocket guide gives the complete picture of modern Dublin food, listing pubs, shops, markets and artisan foods as well as the best restaurants and special places to stay.

ISBN 1 874076 33 2

All Estragon Press titles can be ordered through: bridgestoneguides.com

Also from Estragon Press...

• In this provocative book, John McKenna offers a radical analysis of how restaurants operate, and why some restaurants succeed where others fail.

HOW TO RUN A RESTAURANT

JOHN McKENNA

STRATEGIES FOR SUCCESS IN THE RESTAURANT BUSINESS

• Examining the business from the position of a customer and a critic, McKenna analyses the factors which contribute to success, and explores the decisions which have to be understood by anyone who is either already running a restaurant, or considering opening a new restaurant.

• Practitioners and students will find the book an exhilarating intellectual exploration of one of the most mercurial and fascinating industries and entertainments in the world.

"The McKennas are the most powerful food writing team in the country. They are exciting and talented critics.'

THE SUNDAY BUSINESS POST

NEW from Estragon Press...

Coming in autumn 2001

● The Bridgestone Food Lovers Guide to Ireland: The Traveller's Guide

This is quite a personal book and represents what many people require from the Bridgestone Guides – a concise and vital reference book that tells you in a very accessible format who are the best chefs, who are the best inn keepers, and what are the most delicious local foods that you will find in any and every corner of Ireland.

If used in tandem with the Bridgestone 100 Best Guides, and the Bridgestone Dublin Food Guide, the Bridgestone Food Lovers Guides will help you plan any trip, any holiday and any working engagement, and help you get the best out of Ireland's food and hospitality cultures.

● The Bridgestone Food Lovers Guide to Ireland: The Shopping Guide

In this book you will be able to discover the source of the organic and artisan foods which have revolutionised Ireland's food culture in the last decade. Here are the foods with a human face, foods which are not merely safe, but vital, delicious and indispensible for every Food Lover.

All Estragon Press titles can be ordered through: bridgestoneguides.com